THANK YOU
FOR YOUR SERVICE!

Please accept this book as a gift from our company to you, a respected member of the US Armed Forces.

Bodybuilding.com is grateful for the freedom and protection you provide each day for America.

Your impact on America is incomparable. Use this book as your guide to help transition from the military trenches to the business battlefield. Thank you again from the team at Bodybuilding.com.

BODY BUILDING.com®

Information. Motivation. Supplementation.

IN THE TRENCHES

DO OR DIE LESSONS FROM THE BUSINESS BATTLEFIELD

CRAIG ZUBER

IN THE TRENCHES
DO OR DIE LESSONS FROM THE BUSINESS
BATTLEFIELD

This book was printed in the United States of America.

ISBN 978-0-9826078-0-0

Library of Congress Cataloging-in-Publication Data has been applied for.

CONTENTS

★ ★ ★

This book is dedicated to the brave men and women of the United States armed forces who have served in the past, are currently serving, or will serve in the future, to protect and defend the greatest nation in the world.

It is thanks to their honor, courage, and commitment that we Americans enjoy the opportunity to pursue our dreams of business ownership.

GO TO WWW.SOLDIERSIMPACT.COM!

INTRODUCTION

★ ★ ★

REVEILLE—IT'S GO TIME!

What would you do differently—right now!—
if you knew you were doing it to stay alive?

What does the word "success" mean to you? What are you willing to do to achieve it? What would you do differently—RIGHT NOW—if you knew it was a matter of life or death? Because it is.

Consider this your wake-up call. That's right! Reveille, loud and clear! Get your ass moving and strap on your brain bucket. Not now, but RIGHT NOW. Because running a business IS do or die, black or white, no excuses. No more blaming the economy, your crappy childhood, the government, the fickle public or rotten luck for your business results. The time for blaming and excuses is OVER.

You are the one running this show, you are 100% accountable for wherever your business is right now, and you have the power to achieve any victory you set your mind to, no matter what external forces may be working against you. How? With 100% commitment, a take-no-prisoners attitude, and the discipline to TAKE ACTION and take responsibility every single day of your life.

It's GO TIME.

★★★

The business trenches are littered with the corpses of start-ups that went belly-up—needlessly. Right now, in every city in every state, there are salespeople, consultants, real estate agents, freelancers and professionals in private practice who are working harder than ever but not getting the results they need to stay afloat. They've gone as far as they could on sheer will power, drive, and talent and they're running out of options. They've got the product and/or the expertise to be tops in their field—but they don't know how to set up or run a bulletproof business. *In the Trenches* is packed with the tools, tactics, and battle plans to make it through. How? By applying the life-or-death urgency and precision of a military campaign to the execution of productive business operations. I'm about to show you how to end up raising your colors instead of stuffing a body bag.

BOOT CAMP IN A BOOK

In the chapters to follow, you'll learn how to sell more of your products or services every month, why you need a budget and a business plan and how to use them, the secrets of closing and negotiating, and how to adapt and overcome when ground conditions shift unexpectedly. And that's just for starters. But let me warn you—you're in for one challenging ride.

WARNING

The in-your-face intensity of this book may be too much to digest in one sitting. In the military, they get in your face to save your life. In this book, I get in your face to save your business.

In any branch of the United States Military, your drill sergeants make damn sure you learn how to operate under the most extreme possible conditions. You learn what to do and how to act when mortars, grenades and IEDs are exploding and giving up on your mission is not an option. Hardcore military training is designed to beat skills into your mind and body so completely and so forcefully that you will be able to execute them without hesitation no matter how dire the circumstances. This is training you won't get in a classroom—you learn by experiencing. You learn by doing!

Hardcore military training gets in your face because that is the only way to jolt you into the action that will keep you alive. In this book I will get in your face for exactly the same reason. In 1993 I enlisted in the US Marine Corps to serve the country I love, the best nation on Earth, the land of opportunity where anyone is free to become whatever he or she is determined to be. I wrote this book because I believe absolutely that the entrepreneurial spirit is the engine that powers our greatness. Too many entrepreneurs are wasting that precious opportunity and it's time for that trend to change. Right now. My mission is to make sure your business is the next blockbuster success story, not the next casualty.

If you're a veteran, all the skills you learned in the military are critical for success in the business battlefield—you've learned to persevere and prevail. If you have no military background, *In the Trenches* will show you a completely new way to fire yourself up for dramatically different results in your business, by creating a sense of urgency you may never have experienced before.

It will probably seem like I'm yelling at you; for example, when you come to text in ALL CAPS. I am a driven individual who is very passionate about his mission. So I'm intense. And OK, sometimes I yell. But—like your drill sergeants in boot camp—when I yell, it's for a reason, and one reason only—it's BECAUSE I CARE. I want your business to triumph!

In the Marines I learned to power on to Mission Accomplished at all costs and to never, ever, ever give up. Awesome stuff that served me well in business, with one exception. I took complete charge of my own business, loaded

★ ★ ★
3

everything onto my own back, went for it all out—but I tried to do it all alone. I failed to ask for help. I pulled a John Wayne, and it nearly got me KILLED!

I learned too many lessons the hard way and I want to make damn sure that as many people as possible know the value of asking for help, brainstorming, and learning from others who have gone before. Teamwork is critical. There are plenty of resources out there to use to your advantage that can speed up your success; this book is only one of them.

HOPE IS NOT A BUSINESS BATTLEFIELD TACTIC

The information in this book is not new, it's brain-dead obvious. Most business owners have some idea which things they should be doing to become more profitable. They realize they need business plans, closing skills, self-discipline, and focus. So if they KNOW what they need to do, THEN WHY THE F**K AREN'T THEY DOING IT?

You know why? Because instead of taking action, they rely on "hope."

One of the biggest money-making industries in the world is built on people's hope that they will somehow magically lose weight without doing anything differently. Every week, there's a new diet system or a new approach and consumers jump all over it.

I mean, look, we all know how it works: eat less and get more exercise. EVERYBODY knows this. But because carrying it out would take discipline and commitment, they keep looking for a shortcut or an easier way that gets them washboard abs while they live like couch potatoes.

★ ★ ★

They rely on hope. They hope they can eat half a gallon of ice cream and still wake up three pounds lighter in the morning. They hope they can watch Seinfeld reruns instead of working out and somehow that beer gut will just disappear. Instead of creating and WORKING a business plan, they buy a Powerball ticket.

We are all experts at rationalizing. And we all know the definition of insanity, right? Right. The only way to get different results is to perform new and different ACTIONS. I'm not saying that thinking positive is all wrong—I'm saying that relying on hope alone without exhausting every last shred of energy on every factor within your control is frickin' crazy. It will get you killed.

THERE IS NO "TRY!"

Words have power. And words like "can't" and "if only" and "it'll never happen" and "no" can be crippling weights that keep you crushed in the trenches until your business DIES. So many people are afraid of closing, afraid of asking for what they want, because they might hear the word "no." Is that the end of the world? When someone tells you "no" or "that's not possible," how does that make you feel? Does it fuel your fire or do you accept defeat and quit? How long do you think "no" is good for, anyway? I can tell you from many years of experience that "no" is only good for about five minutes. In a business context, "no" is just a momentary setback that makes the game more interesting, not a permanent answer. Getting a "no" answer doesn't mean it's over, it means you now have an excellent opportunity to ask different questions, better questions, and LISTEN to the answers until you learn what it will take to get to "yes."

Another word that has no place in the business battlefield vocabulary is "try." Yoda had it right when he told Luke Skywalker "There is no "try!" You either do it or you fail to do it.

★ ★ ★

Whenever you say you'll try to accomplish something, you're setting yourself up to fail by giving yourself an excuse for it not to work. In business, nobody cares whether you tried. Did you do it or not? All the excuses in the world won't make any difference if you're dead.

A very close relative of "I'll try" is "someday," also known as "tomorrow." Tomorrow never comes! Why do you think they have "Free crabs tomorrow!" posted all over the outside of every Crab Shack restaurant in the country? That's why we will not talk about goal setting. Instead, we'll make AND KEEP specific commitments.

A goal is just *hope* in disguise. If you set a goal to "get in shape," what exactly does that mean? What will happen next? Probably nothing. But if you make and keep a commitment to get up at 5:30 a.m. five days a week and go to the gym before going to work, you will soon see tangible, measurable results.

THE BEST AND WORST DAY OF MY LIFE

When I entered the United States Marine Corps and put on that uniform, a feeling of strength came to me, as if I had become the master of my own destiny. And that feeling was tested almost beyond what I could bear the day they took me and 11 other recruits to "the beach." Trust me, you do not want to be on a Marine Corps beach! Sergeant Smith and Staff Sergeant Morris had decided this was the day to weed out the quitters. So far, their efforts had been highly effective—my platoon started with 115 recruits and only 75 of us graduated.

It was hotter than a snake's ass that day. In deep sand and off-the-map humidity, they put us through drill after drill. I have never heard the word "ZUBER!" yelled so many times in one day. Sergeant Smith had me double time in place for what felt like an hour, side-straddle hop until my feet went numb, and do Marine Corps pushups until every muscle in my arms, chest, and back gave out. Then it was flip over and do lying leg lifts six inches off the ground until my abdomen, heart, and lungs felt like they were about to explode.

Sound tough? You have no idea. Especially because I was still reeling from what felt like a near-death experience earlier that same day—the "gas chamber."

As a training exercise, we had been exposed to a non-lethal but still toxic gas known as "CS gas" (chlorobenzylidene malonitrile). In a small room filled with it, they told us to take off our gas masks and recite our social security numbers over and over. Within minutes, every one of us felt like we were surely DYING. With every breath, every part of my body inside and out burned until I was soon regurgitating everything in my system. When there was nothing left, that changed to dry heaves. The snot and tears were streaming down my face, completely outside my control. Grown men were jumping around like kangaroos, screaming and bawling like newborns. My eyes were sizzling in my head—I was convinced I'd be blind if I even got out of there alive.

But I did survive! Without being blinded, and without giving up! OOH-RAH!

There was no time for relief, however; because next thing I knew I was straining on "the beach," sweating so hard that a puddle the size of Lake Erie was forming in the sand under my body. "Blow into the sand and get it in your neck and eyes and ears, Zuber!" yelled Sergeant Smith. "Just QUIT! All you have to do is quit and this will all be over!"

I suddenly realized a priceless truth. Even in unbearable conditions with the voice of authority screaming at me to "Just

★ ★ ★

QUIT!" the choice about whether to go on or give up was mine alone. I chose to hold on, no matter what. And I made it through.

Sergeant Smith looked me in the eye and said, "Zuber, no matter what happens in life from here on out, *nothing will ever be harder than this day.* When you're stressed out and the world feels like it's caving in around you, you'll be able to look back on this and laugh! You didn't quit. You never gave up."

I knew then if I could make it through that day, I could make it through anything. I learned that the only person who could make me quit—was me. And the only person who can make YOU quit is YOU.

READING THIS IS NOT ENOUGH

Buying this book will not get you out of the trenches. Even reading it isn't enough. You've got to use it and work it. Getting to Mission Accomplished takes a no-excuses commitment to bold, decisive ACTION, every day. That commitment is your job.

I can tell you what to do, I can give you the inspiration, the information, the ideas, and the tactics – but I will not be around to personally haul your ass out of bed in the morning and get you moving. To make your business a success and get out of the trenches alive, you've got to keep showing up. It takes guts to go for it without stopping until you succeed at being the best you can be. It's up to you to lead the team. It's up to you to face the facts. It's up to you to rise to the challenges and do whatever it takes to WIN on the business battlefield.

You're the one driving this train and you're the only one who can make it go in a new direction.

★ ★ ★

REVEILLE TOP 3 TAKEAWAYS

1. Running a business is a matter of life or death—it's DO OR DIE.
2. *Hope* is not a business tactic. Results follow ACTION, not *hope*.
3. Strap on your brain bucket, because it's GO TIME!

YOUR MARCHING ORDERS

1. Answer these questions:
   a. What is your definition of success?
   b. What, specifically, are you willing to do to achieve it?
   c. What is one thing you can start doing differently in your business—right now?
2. Take the answer to that last question and DO IT within 24 hours. No excuses.

★ ★ ★

RAISE YOUR COLORS

★ ★ ★

NOTHING HAPPENS
WITHOUT THE CLOSE!

*If you're not closing, you're not selling. And if you're not selling,
then you are not in business.*

On February 23, 1945, a handful of Marines climbed to the top of
Mount Suribachi in Iwo Jima, Japan. After four days of fighting
like hell and heavy casualties, they were not gaining any ground.
Raising the flag was Sergeant Mike Strank's idea. He hand-
picked five guys and took them up that mountain to raise the
United States flag high enough "so that every Marine on this
cruddy island can see it."

You've probably heard this story, because the photograph of
five Marines and one Navy Corpsman raising their colors is one of
the most reproduced images in history. It's an amazing shot. And
what's even more amazing is that they did eventually win, against
incredible odds and at great cost. It took 32 more days after the
flag went up, but somehow the sight of it waving proudly above
the smoke and shrapnel carried a loud and clear message: "We
will prevail. We WILL make this happen, no matter what it
takes." They believed.

★★★

In battle, it takes unshakeable determination to achieve victory. On the business battlefield, achieving victory means closing.

This chapter will discuss when to close, how to close and why to close. You'll get an insider's analysis of what's really going on in every business interaction. Doing business successfully means closing everyone, all of the time, while you are educating, communicating, marketing and negotiating.

Closing is about searching for YES questions during the entire process of every business transaction. And then when the timing is right: ASK. FOR. THE. ORDER.

In the business trenches, nothing happens without the close.

CLOSING TACTIC #1

Tell your prospects a story about a past client who was feeling the same reservations they're feeling right now, but who decided to go ahead with the deal and as a result is now much better off and very glad they made the right choice.

CLOSING DEFINED

When I say close, I'm not talking about closing up shop and calling it a day! I'm talking about making a deal and getting to "yes." Closing means getting a commitment to move forward, to purchase, to sign, to stay or to go. And it doesn't necessarily always mean making a sale.

Sometimes closing is a matter of getting the other party to commit to taking the next step—whether it's writing the check, signing the contract, making an appointment, or even agreeing to the next meeting.

★ ★ ★

Closing successfully is really about creating a relationship that will lead to multiple commitments to buy more of your products or services. You've seen it a million times. An experienced waiter is constantly closing all through the meal by selling you more appetizers, more cocktails, and more desserts. A business coach closes by getting a new client to commit to that first appointment and then getting them to sign up for a six-month contract.

SHOW UP LOCKED AND LOADED

The best insurance you can have for a successful close is being well prepared. Do your homework. Being prepared is what makes the difference between closing and losing. You need to be able to answer questions, deal knowledgeably with any issues that come up, and instill confidence that you know what you're doing.

Arm yourself with an arsenal of questions that will help you learn exactly what motivates them and what they're looking for so that you can demonstrate exactly how your product or service is the answer to their prayers. Have a crystal clear explanation ready of all the benefits they'll enjoy by moving forward and all the negative consequences of missing this opportunity. Make sure you're totally up to date and informed about what's going on in your market and your industry—as well as their market and their industry.

The more information you have ready, the better you'll be able to think on your feet and deal with any surprises or obstacles.

EVERYBODY WINS. NO EXCEPTIONS.

Your goal in closing is not just a one-time sale. What you're looking for is a long-term working relationship that will lead to more business. It is a LOT more expensive to court new customers than to keep the ones you already have. By making

★ ★ ★

every close result in a win-win outcome, you keep customers happy. When you create an enjoyable and rewarding experience for your clients, they look forward to doing business with you again and again. Closing them gets easier with every transaction, because they grow to trust you.

This is where closing is different than negotiation. In negotiation, the outcome is not always a win/win, but in closing it has to be. If you come out of a transaction feeling like you won and the other party did not, you've just lost. You will never have repeat business for the rest of your career from these people. They will never refer you business, either. Nothing else is going to happen after that one-time shot. What kind of triumph is that?

Winning is a matter of creating happy customers, who not only buy from you but also tell their friends about you and send referrals. There is no better advertising on the planet than a testimonial from a satisfied customer.

CLOSING TACTIC #2

Restate the long list of benefits your clients have just disclosed as important to them and list them in order of priority. This tactic confirms and reinforces in your prospect's mind all of the valid reasons for moving forward..

THE OPENING

A huge part of closing is "opening." The way you get the conversation started is the first step in setting up the close. It's all about the presentation and the delivery, the way you ask your questions, and making sure everyone is comfortable. Tell a simple joke. For example, ask them the minute you meet them if they brought a suitcase full of cash and are ready to move forward. Find a way to connect with them as people and make them laugh. When they are comfortable, you will be comfortable,

★ ★ ★

and when you are comfortable it makes asking for the order much easier.

The warm-up stage is also a great opportunity to find out who the decision maker is. If you're working with a couple, pay attention to their body language and notice who always has the last word. Sometimes you can simply come right out and ask, or you can test the waters by asking in a joking way. In some cases, it may be a touchy subject. If you're in a one-on-one meeting, get it out on the table before getting started whether the person you're with is authorized to make decisions and move forward today or they have to clear it with somebody else.

Watch the body language to verify—they might tell you the husband is the decider, but if you and he start deciding things and the wife is shifting uncomfortably in her seat or looking concerned, you need to adjust.

Why is that important? Because if I'm communicating with 100% clarity to Mr. Smith and rarely focusing on Mrs. Smith, and Mrs. Smith is the decision maker, how far do you think I'm going to get when it's time to close? Nowhere! Mrs. Smith will be frustrated and she'll take that frustration out on Mr. Smith afterwards and together those two are going to come up with the idea that I'm not the right person to work with.

NEVER EVER ASSUME!

Time after time I've heard new recruits tell me they know just how to adjust their approach to a potential customer based on how the person dresses, what kind of watch they wear, how old they are, or how wealthy they appear to be. And that's bullshit.

Why? Because whether or not somebody buys from you has absolutely nothing to do with what they're wearing or how they act. It has everything to do with the questions you ask and how

★ ★ ★

well you listen to their response, taking that information and using it as leverage to lead them in the right direction.

Never assume that someone is or is not going to buy based on your own knee-jerk impression of them. Trying to close too soon can backfire rapidly, and it's always the result of assuming the client is ready when they're not. Don't assume! Listen! If you're not sure, ask!

Prejudging isn't the only way assumptions will get you killed. Have you ever lost a customer because they were expecting a follow-up call, which you didn't make because you had no idea that's what they were expecting? A professional refuses to leave things hanging.

Every time you talk to a customer or a prospect (or anyone, really), it's your responsibility to make sure both parties leave the meeting or phone call knowing what is going to happen next and who is expected to do what. And that means closing, because you're not going to leave that meeting with only a "maybe" for an answer. You're going to get a commitment.

Even in cases where you're not actually closing on a sale, you still need to be closing them on something. Instead of saying, "I'll get back to you," say when. If they say, "I'm not sure," get a commitment on the specific date and time you will contact them to get their decision.

DON'T WAIT UNTIL THE END TO CLOSE

Closing is a process, not a step. When you meet with a client or prospect, you are continually helping them get more comfortable with you and more excited about the possibilities. Continually asking the right clarifying questions and working toward getting approval helps set the stage for you to ask for the order as the next logical part of the progression.

★ ★ ★

- ★ Are you OK with the price?
- ★ How do you feel about the service; have we met your expectations?
- ★ Is this product/service what you need?
- ★ Do you see yourself owning/using this product/service and how it will make your life easier?
- ★ Do you have any concerns?

It's a matter of always leading up to the next step, and getting small commitments—"yes" answers—along the way. If you're just shooting the breeze and talking about whatever for an hour and then suddenly try to close during the last five minutes, that becomes very uncomfortable for both parties. By the time you ask for the order, it should feel like a natural progression because you have been closing all along.

CLOSING TACTIC #3

Take your prospects back to the property or hand them the product and let them use it or experience it and picture themselves having it. This tactic helps the prospect become emotionally attached.

All communication should be laying the groundwork for the close, always.

CONFIDENCE BREEDS CONFIDENCE

The military approach to business is based solidly on courage and confidence. If you are not completely confident about your product or service or your ability to deliver it—fix that now. And I mean RIGHT NOW. No excuses.

Your confidence comes from your absolute belief that what you're offering is truly the right thing for them to do. If it isn't, NEVER push someone into buying something they shouldn't.

★ ★ ★

Closing is supposed to be about pushing them into buying something they should.

Sometimes business people are so intimidated by the close that they project desperation, but closing doesn't need to be like that. The trick is to create an enjoyable experience—the close should be fun. It's supposed to be a step everyone will be celebrating about before, during, and after.

It works because of your confidence, your unshakable faith that your product or service is the best. It also works because of your sincerity. You are genuinely looking out for their best interests and they will be able to see, hear and feel that. On the other hand, if you're only out for yourself at their expense—you're DEAD! It will show, every time.

Here's the bottom line: if you're intimidated about closing—GET OVER IT. Learning to close is not optional, it is mandatory. The secret? Believe in your mind that you already have the client's approval to proceed and act accordingly.

CREATE A SENSE OF URGENCY

Creating a sense of urgency is do or die. You've established all the excellent reasons to move forward and the obvious value of what your customers will get from your product or service. You know they want to do this. You know and they know that it's the right move for them and that it's in their best interests.

But if they're not ready to close, you're still not done educating. You need to make clear to them everything they stand to lose by not closing today. Right now, because it's GO TIME. This is where being prepared comes in handy once again. Let's say you're a real estate agent and your buyers are hesitating. What are the compelling reasons for them to act now? Maybe market conditions are changing, interest rates are going up, things are selling quicker, or it looks as if the opportunity will not be around

★ ★ ★

tomorrow. If none of these tactics work—then get them to move forward today by offering a 100% bulletproof, absolutely nothing-to-lose way out of the deal.

For example, you might say, "If I can find you the perfect property, in the right location, that meets all of your standards and your price point, are you prepared to move forward?" If the answer to that question is a NO, then the next question is "What will it take for you to move forward today? Were you aware that two other buyers are interested in the property and you might lose out on this AMAZING opportunity if we wait too long?"

Create a sense of excitement! Make it feel like a celebration. Paint a picture that illustrates how they have nothing to lose and everything to gain by acting NOW.

ASK FOR THE ORDER

It's astounding how many business people and salespeople skip this step. Closing the deal MUST include asking for the order. If you do all of the legwork, schedule meetings, put on presentations and pitches and spell out the benefits—but you fail to ask for the order or get a signature—your business is DEAD!

Asking for money can sometimes be difficult, even for the best sales people. But that can be overcome with the proper preparation and delivery. Make it fun and exciting. Make it a vital point to find the value to your prospect in your services or your product and then focus in on all the benefits for them and get them excited. And then Ask. For. The. Order.

The funny thing is that so many people are afraid to ask for the order because they're afraid of that "no." But you will be amazed at how many times people will say "yes." Let's say you're on a phone call with a prospect and you've just learned what you're prospect is looking for and made a beautiful case for how your service is just right for them, and there's a lull in the conversation. Instead of just waiting to see what happens, say, "Let's set an appointment right now. I'm available on Tuesday at 2:00 pm." It's highly probable you'll get a "yes."

If you never ask, you'll never hear "no," but you'll never hear "yes," either. You know that line about missing 100% of the shots you don't take? That's the point. So just do it. Ask for the f***ing order.

KNOW WHEN TO WALK AWAY

Even if you do everything right, you will sometimes find yourself in a situation that's going nowhere. An experienced closer can tell from the earliest questions when they're faced with a customer who is not likely to close, ever. Or there's the case of a potential client who keeps wasting your time in meeting after meeting, but just never seems to commit.

That's when you need to evaluate how valuable your time is. Maybe you've done all you could to create a sense of urgency and the perfect scenario to meet their needs, but they're still not ready to move. You've asked the question in a dozen different ways and the answer is still no.

The fact is, people drag themselves through the wringer because they refuse to close or commit to any decision. When that keeps happening with a client, it's time to step back. Let them know tactfully but definitively that it's not worth wasting any more of their time or yours. Ask them what would be the purpose of getting together for another meeting, if we're not going to make anything happen?

Never try to close when you aren't feeling it – your GUT is actually your heart attached to your brain – and it's very rarely wrong. So listen to it! If you feel it's not going to happen, if there's a personality conflict, or your product just isn't a fit for

★ ★ ★

them and it will most likely never be a win-win for both parties – then STOP what you are doing. Kill them with kindness and send them on their merry way! Focus your energy on people who value your service and your product and stop wasting your energy on people who don't.

CLOSING TACTIC #4

On paper, make a list of all the pros and cons. (But first, make damn sure there are more pros than cons!) Draw a line down the center of a page and start filling up the "pros" section. This tactic is excellent with "A" type personalities.

BEWARE OF THE HARD CLOSE

The classic example of bad salesmanship is the cliché of the used car dealer. Just reading that, you're probably cringing and gritting your teeth, the hair on your neck stands up and you're making a face—but why? Because everybody "knows" that used car dealers are just in it for themselves. They are like sharks. You get out of your car and they're on you in 30 seconds. And there's no getting around it.

Even if you go to the dealership having done all your research and you know exactly what you want to buy and how much you're willing to pay, you still have to go through a decidedly unpleasant experience with one of these dickheads to get the car.

When you finally get it over with, are you ever going to refer anyone to the salesman who subjected you to the shark attack? No. Did you enjoy that experience? No. No relationship was created, the experience was awful—so even though he made the sale, did the car dealer win? He didn't. His one-shot "win" actually cut off any future opportunities with you.

★ ★ ★

If you try to sell people instead of listening to them, educating them, and respecting them, you will lose many more deals than you close. More importantly, you'll lose the opportunity to build a lasting, profitable, enjoyable working relationship.

FOCUS ON THE VALUE, NOT THE MONEY

Too many closings fail because both parties get stuck in the vortex of haggling over the price. But it doesn't have to be that way. The secret is to keep the conversation focused on what they are getting, not what they are spending.

It's all about value. What is their need? How is your offering going to fulfill that need? What have they lost out on in the past? Stay focused and never let your clients miss the many ways they can truly benefit from your service. You do that by educating them on the reasons for moving forward, explaining the upsides of making the decision right now. STOP focusing on the money; it will get you killed every time. Start focusing on all of the positive reasons on why your client deserves your services and how much enjoyment they will receive in return.

CLOSING TAKES PRACTICE

No two people close in exactly the same way. My bride Nicole and I are both great at closing. We each get results; however, our styles are completely different. Everyone has their own style and their own approach, and that's something that takes practice to develop. There is a learning curve, but you learn by feeling it out and paying attention to what works and what doesn't.

I could say, here's how I do it, and give you a word-for-word script—but you're not me. I can't tell you what to do every time, because the next time you close, I won't be there. To give you an exact script, I'd need to know your prospect's personality profile.

★ ★ ★

I'd have to observe how they've been treating the questions, whether they were happy at first and now they're not, or whether they have been uptight the entire time.

To learn what to say—practice. What you can do to improve is debrief yourself—preferably with a skilled closer or a business coach—after every close. Dissect what went down and consider how you might have done it differently. What if you tried this? Or maybe that? What was something that felt right and worked great and how can you make that happen again?

The best way to learn how to close is by DOING IT. So get out there in the trenches and start closing.

KEEP LISTENING

That arsenal of questions you've walked in with won't do anybody any good unless you really pay attention to the answers. What are they really looking for in life? What is their burning desire or greatest fear? How do they envision themselves, who do they want to be when they grow up, and how can whatever you're selling make that vision a reality for them?

To choose the right closing tactics in any situation, you need to have a good handle on the kind of personality you're dealing with. The way they answer your questions—or what's between the lines of the questions they ask you—is full of valuable clues to their personality profile.

Your clients and prospects will tell you everything you need to know to close them on whatever you're selling. I guarantee it. Keep your eyes and ears open and pay attention to what your gut tells you. Notice everything. If you can out-listen your prospects well enough, they will practically close themselves!

★ ★ ★

CLOSING TACTIC #5

If you know they are almost ready to buy, but they're still hesitating, take it away from them. Suggest convincingly that what you're offering is no longer available or may not be the right fit for them—and watch their expressions. This tactic helps get prospects off the fence.

OVERCOMING OBJECTIONS

The best way to handle objections is to prevent them from coming up in the first place.

For example, if you've asked enough questions to establish what they really want, what their price point is, and how important this deal is to them, that makes it tough for them to suddenly insist that the price is too high. It's too late for that; you've already had that discussion.

But it's natural for people to feel resistance or fear, especially if whatever you're closing them on is a big step outside their comfort zone. Objections can give you a great opportunity to help them talk it through and get more comfortable with their decision.

Always be respectful. Ask questions on a different subject or make a joke to change the mood. And then, get back to educating them—this time from a different angle they may not have thought about before.

There are several typical objections that come up during a close. Here are some tactics for handling them.

★ "I can't afford it," or "Your price is too high." Be confident in your service and your product. Ask the question "How could we work it out so that you could

★ ★ ★
24

afford it?" Be creative. Would financing work? Installment payments? One warning here: trying to sell them something they truly cannot afford is unethical and will come back to haunt you every time.

★ "I need to think about it" or "Not now, but call me again in the fall." What will be different in the fall? What do they stand to lose by waiting? If there is a compelling reason to buy today, explain it.

★ "I need to check with [some other person] to get the go-ahead." The best way to deal with this curve ball is to find out who the decision maker is, right up front, at the beginning of the conversation. Nips this one in the bud!

★ "I just can't make up my mind." Create a "what if" scenario for both doing it and not doing it. Or ask the question, "We can go around and around on this all day, but the overall question is: what is it going to take for you to move forward today?"

TIMING IS EVERYTHING

How do you know when to ask for the order? You feel it. You can read it in their body language. You can sense whether you are getting along well and building up rapport—especially when you're consistently getting "yes" answers.

Feel out whether it's time with questions like, "Are you comfortable with the process so far?" "How are you feeling about this?" "If we can get this for this price, are you excited?" When they are saying yes to those things, it's time to say "Let's put this on paper right now because you have nothing to lose."

KNOW WHEN TO SHUT UP

Once a prospect has committed to moving forward – SHUT UP! And get it in writing as quickly as possible. This will eliminate any opportunity for second thoughts, and you'll be rewarding them with the relief of having the process DONE. No more

★ ★ ★

haggling. No more thinking so hard. No more having to hear you jabber on.

The power of the pen is incredible; however, if you keep talking after the pen comes out, you can still screw it all up.

CLOSING TACTIC #6

Break the purchase down into payments, so your customers can focus on a smaller number instead of one large lump sum. This tactic works well when pricing and interest rates are going up.

THE BOTTOM LINE

Closing is the most important aspect of selling. And you can do it. Go out on a limb and ask for the order. Leave your safety blanket behind and just do it. Get a commitment. Make the sale.

When it works—and it WILL work—you'll experience the power of getting to "yes." You'll approach every meeting with a clear goal in mind, locked and loaded with answers to potential objections and plenty of the right questions to ask that will keep the process flowing. No more wasted appointments where nothing is accomplished. No more stalemates. Closing will soon become a habit and you will taste the thrill of making great things happen.

★ ★ ★

RAISE YOUR COLORS TOP 5 TAKEAWAYS

1. All communication is laying the groundwork for the close, always.
2. Your clients and prospects will tell you everything you need to know to close them on whatever you're selling. LISTEN!
3. Don't wait till the end to close.
4. Closing is the single most important aspect of selling.
5. Ask for the order!

YOUR MARCHING ORDERS

Go to your contacts database and find a would-be client or prospect who has been on the fence or stringing you along for months without being willing to say "yes" or "no." Call them up and close them. Get them to commit to something—even if it's only an appointment—or cut them from your list.

★ ★ ★

PLATOON SERGEANT

★ ★ ★

BECOMING A LEADER WHO WINS IN THE TRENCHES!

"When we step on the battlefield,
mine will be the first boots on and the last boots off."
– *Lieutenant General Hal Moore*

Leaders don't sit around waiting or *hoping* for something to happen—leaders MAKE amazing things happen! Instead of excuses or blame, leaders deliver solutions and results. Leaders go above and beyond the call of duty. Doing a good job is not enough—leaders push themselves to greatness. Anyone at any level can be a leader by stepping up and taking initiative.

Leaders influence and inspire others by actions, not by words, and work to achieve specific results by working collaboratively with others. They are more concerned with the success of the team than their own personal gain. And, leadership doesn't just apply to your troops—your clients are also counting on you to be the expert who will guide them through unfamiliar territory by protecting and advancing their best interests.

LEADERSHIP MEANS SERVICE

There's a stereotype out there that when you get to be the boss you get to put your feet up on the desk, clamp a cigar between

★ ★ ★

your teeth, and order people around. The boss reaps the profits while the grunts do all the work, right? Wrong. Making a business work is a team effort, not a one-man show. Even if you're a sole proprietor, you've still got to have a team; what about your vendors, your clients, your mentors, your CPA, your spouse and family, your colleagues, and/or your coach or mastermind group?

In a team, everybody has a job to do, and the leader's job is to get results and to steer the business wisely so that it prospers and provides services for customers and a place to work for the employees. And barking out orders is not the way to prosperity— teamwork is.

Do you open staff meetings by saying, "Here's what we're going to do, because I say so, period." or by saying, "Here's the situation. What do you think? How can we solve this?" There's a leader trait. Ask people what they think and listen to them.

True leaders understand and leverage the power of A.L.L.—Ask, Listen, and Learn. It's ALL or nothing.

Power can be a heady thing, and it's easy to fall into the trap of believing you know everything and you're always right. But leaders who allow that to happen are heading for disaster.

Business is service-oriented, no matter what industry you're in. The best way to lead is by continually improving the service you provide, to your people and your customers.

Ask any highly successful manager or CEO how they run such a top-flight operation and I guarantee you'll hear something like this: "I just hire really, really good people and then stay out of their way." Or, "It's my people who do all the work, I just make sure they have everything they need to do it right." Organization development experts even have a name for this; they call it "servant leadership." And it WORKS.

★ ★ ★

These are the kind of leaders who consistently attract and retain the best of the best when it comes to staff, the kind of leaders people will follow right into the valley of death without question or hesitation.

COMMANDER IN TENT—LEADERSHIP IN THE TRENCHES

In the field and in the trenches, the leader is always easy to identify. They'll be the first one over the barricade leading the charge. And their troops will be right beside them 100% with absolute trust and commitment. How does a leader win that kind of trust? By making it 100% clear that you've got their back. Not just saying it—but SHOWING IT!

Beneath the Marine Corps approach to motivating Marines to achieve a desired result is the simple principle that true leadership is leading from the front. This means first showing the effort and making the sacrifice that the Platoon Sergeant is asking of his Marines. It means a willingness to perform above and beyond the call of duty and share the same conditions as his Marines – no matter how miserable or trivial the task. This principle echoes throughout the entire organization - inspiring greater performance at all levels and creating unquestionable trust in the leader – through actions, not words.

You're in combat training and you're on a 15-mile hump with 70+ pounds on your back on a 90-degree day with 90% humidity. You're heading up a 25-degree slope and everybody is practically dying and somebody falls back. Do you leave them? Do you scream at them? No, not if you're a true leader. You get out of the line, go back for that soldier, and help push them up the hill, because we all make it across the line or nobody makes it across the line.

★ ★ ★

In the military, you never leave your wingman. Ever notice when warplanes are flying, there is always two or three of them at a time? Nobody flies alone.

WHY LEADERSHIP MATTERS

Without leadership, nothing gets done. What happens if nobody steps up? Nothing. Somebody has to cross the bridge first, to be the one who sticks their neck out, to establish a direction and inspire people to action.

Anyone can lead from any level—opportunities to be a leader are everywhere, every day. What does that mean? It means step up, take charge. If you see that something clearly needs to be done, why are you waiting for somebody else to do it? Say, for example, I'm working in my cube and I realize that a system isn't working right and I have an idea for making it better. But, I'm not the boss, so I don't speak up or stick my neck out. That's crazy!

You might say, "Well, what if the boss feels threatened?" But a great leader welcomes ideas. A great leader WANTS someone to come to him or her with a solution instead of a problem. To become a leader you must actively seek out new challenges. Take every opportunity for increased responsibility and perform every task, large or small, to the best of your ability. Your reward will come in the form of opportunities to take on bigger, more important projects. Especially if, in the absence of direction, you take the initiative to proceed with the action you believe will get the best results.

Leaders do not have the luxury of giving in to panic or despair. It takes courage, honesty, and most importantly—discipline, as in the ability to control your impulses and stay calm and cool under pressure. Remember that old saying about keeping your head while everyone around you is losing theirs? That's leadership. Instead of hitting the panic button and

★ ★ ★

yelling, "We're all gonna die!" a leader steps back, takes stock of the situation, and says, "OK. How can we fix this?"

Emergencies happen. Have you ever been in an office environment when the Internet went down? People freak out. You'd think it was the end of the world. But seriously, does a temporary technical difficulty mean your entire business just fell apart?

A leader takes a different approach. A leader says, "Let's look at our options here. Who can we call and what's the fastest way to fix it?" and, "What can each of us do to keep operating in the meantime?"

A leader thinks things through. When someone on your team comes to you so frustrated that they want to take action right now and do potentially all the wrong things, you're the voice of reason who listens to them with respect and is willing to say, "Let's think about this. What should we do that would be best for the company? For the big picture?"

That approach pays off in multiple ways—you prevent an outcome that could damage the business. You win the trust and buy-in of an employee instead of turning them into an adversary. And you set an example of what leadership is supposed to look like.

VALUE YOUR PEOPLE

It's mind-blowing to see the results a great leader can get by placing a high value on people and treating them well—and that means treating them with respect! And it also means making the effort to get to know who they are as people and what's important to them. It means paying attention and learning what they need from you to get their job done and give their best.

★ ★ ★

If you think that sounds like too much work and too much wasted time, think again. Think about how disruptive it is to you and everybody else when an employee or partner leaves. And what a pain in the ass it is to interview new people, recruit a replacement, bring them up to speed, and then find out the hard way whether they're up to the task. Don't forget that this all goes on during time you could have been spending selling or producing or generating new customers. When you look at how much it costs in both time and money to let people go and bring new people on board, the ROI of investing the time in keeping the good ones is HUGE.

A lot of it has to do with personality profiles, because different people have different motivations for what they do well. I know that Dennis thrives on competition, so I make sure he gets competition in his work. Nicole is motivated by appreciation; she needs to know, often, that she's doing a great job and that we all appreciate it. Everybody is driven by something different. And it's your job as a leader to figure out what that is.

When you're a true leader, you take responsibility for clear, two-way communication with your team so they know exactly what you expect of them. You stand up for them and make sure they have the resources and support they need to fulfill their mission.

We all need respect. And we all need chances to learn and grow and stretch ourselves. And sometimes that means failing. A very critical part of great leadership involves trusting your people to use their own judgment, because that builds their confidence and decision-making skills. The flip side of that is that you have to give them permission to fail. Failure is an inescapable part of learning; so if they do make a mistake, treat it as a learning opportunity. Instead of ripping their head off, you talk about what they could have done differently, or what you might have

★ ★ ★

done in their place to get a different result. You take on the responsibility for whatever happened, because you're the one who gave them permission to fail. Then you go the extra mile and take responsibility for seeing it through. You help everybody learn from the mistake.

But leadership isn't only about when things go south—team spirit grows from rewarding hard work and setting benchmarks that tell you when you're making progress so you can celebrate! We'd all rather be congratulated than get our asses kicked, right? Small steps are worth making a fuss about. Small steps are just fine, as long as they're going in the right direction. And celebrations must include everybody—everybody needs to be included as a team. There's no "I" did it, there's always "we" did it.

INSTILLING CONFIDENCE

When I began working on this book, my son Zac asked me, "Why are you always carrying that note pad around, Dad?" I told him I was writing a book, and he got it, and he liked the idea. In fact, he liked it so much he decided he wanted to write a book, too (he's six). So then we were both carrying note pads around all the time.

OK, almost all the time. One day we were at the beach playing in the surf when I got this phrase in my head that I knew I wanted in the book. Neither one of us had our notebooks or anything to write with.

So I asked Zac if he could help me do something really important for my book. I asked him to remember a few words of a certain key phrase and we recited it back and forth until he had the words down cold. He was all over it—he was thrilled to be included and to know that I was counting on him.

★ ★ ★

When we got back to the hotel room, the second I picked up a pen and notepad he immediately fired off not just the key words, but the whole phrase. All I had to do was write it down. He was so excited! He didn't need a treat or a tip or a prize—all the reward he needed was the knowledge that his dad's book would have a message inside that wouldn't have been possible without him. He was included! He contributed! I had depended on him and he delivered! OOH-RAH!

It was an awesome moment, and that's what leadership is all about. No business is a one-man show. The people who work with you, and for you, want to feel included and they want to excel. They need opportunities to shine, to be heard, and to make contributions that make a difference. They need to hear you say, "Great job!" and know without any doubt that you mean it and you're absolutely right.

SHOW, DON'T TELL

Leading by example isn't one way to lead; it's the only way. As the leader in the trenches, your duty is to set the tone and set the standard for the team by your actions and personal example. If your attitude, focus, appearance, and performance are consistently held to the highest standard, you can rightfully demand the same of your team. But if your own personal standards are poor or inconsistent, you'll be setting a double standard for your team and you will lose their respect and confidence—RAPIDLY.

Show your team that you're willing to do the same things you ask them to do. Conduct yourself so that your personal habits are above reproach. Share danger and hardship with your team to demonstrate your willingness to carry your share and more. Develop a logical and orderly thought process by practicing objective estimation of the situation and sharing your reasoning with the team. People are much more likely to support an

★ ★ ★

objective if they know the "why" behind it and they trust your objectivity.

And always remember—courage is contagious!

KEEP A RESPECTFUL DISTANCE

Being the boss can be an isolating experience sometimes. It's not possible to be everyone's buddy when you're the leader, nor does it really serve the business or the people you're responsible for. So remember to be careful about getting too close to the people you are leading! Your duty is to make the tough decisions when necessary, and that includes decisions that affect whether people lose their jobs or get bonuses.

Own your decisions—and accept responsibility for them. If you make a mistake, admit it and change course. People respect leaders who correct mistakes immediately for the good of the business instead of bluffing their way through a poor decision to protect their egos.

REMEMBER WHO'S FLYING THE PLANE

When Larry Laraway was a First Lieutenant in the Air Force, he learned a hard lesson that changed the way he flew his plane and kept him alive flying through hostile territory in North Vietnam. He brought that lesson home with him and has been applying it ever since on the business battlefield.

He was getting prepared to upgrade from Co-Pilot to Pilot on a B-52 Bomber. The evaluation instructor let Laraway know that he better know all of the emergency procedures better than he knew his own mother and nail them all or the instructor would fail him. No questions, no excuses!

★ ★ ★

Laraway studied hard until he knew the emergency procedures inside and out, forward and backwards. He was more than prepared for his check ride when the day came. He and the evaluation instructor took off and leveled out at 30,000 feet. Then, Laraway put the B-52 on autopilot and spent the next 40 minutes going through all of the emergency procedures, in the correct order and sequence, with total concentration.

After Laraway had completed all the required tasks, the evaluator let Laraway know that what he had just performed was one of the greatest jobs the evaluator had ever seen. With only one problem—the plane had crashed and they were dead!

Laraway had been so focused on completing the emergency procedures flawlessly that he never took time to check whether the plane was still on the right flight path. As part of the test, early on during Laraway's drill the evaluator had reached over and tweaked the autopilot just slightly. After 40 minutes of nobody checking it, that slight tweak had moved the plane off it's heading by 15 degrees. If the plane had continued on the wrong heading, that 15 degree error would have been enough to send it crashing into a mountainside instead of safely reaching the landing strip.

The moral of the story? You may be able to handle all of the emergencies in the world, but you still have to fly the airplane. If you quit flying the airplane—you're dead!

It's no different in life or business. You may have developed the best systems and trained the best people—but you still have to run the business. If you let yourself get too comfortable flying on autopilot, you will fail to notice that slight degree of variance sending you off course in time to adjust it. Your business will be DEAD before you know what hit you.

★ ★ ★

LEADERS DEVELOP LEADERS

Alexander the Great supposedly said, "An army of sheep led by a lion is greater than an army of lions led by a sheep." And I'll agree that the pack of sheep led by a lion will knock the shit out of a pack of lions led by a sheep.

But what if you had a pack of lions led by a lion? You and your team would be unstoppable. So why wouldn't everybody figure out a way to create a team of leaders?

A few pages ago, we talked about how great leaders welcome ideas and appreciate it when somebody speaks up with a solution. Unfortunately, not all leaders get this. We've all worked for somebody at one time or another in our lives who was a control freak. What drives me most crazy about that situation is that these people are sabotaging their own businesses by missing out on all that creativity and innovation!

If you're leading people effectively, you'll be excited when they step up instead of intimidated that they might take over your role. If you are getting people to ACT instead of sitting back on their asses waiting for you to tell them every move to make—then you're doing it right! Yes, there are times when you need to take control and have the final say. But wouldn't you rather have people around you who are taking action, in motion, instead of going to sleep? You need other leaders to back you up. You need to trust your team if you expect them to trust you. And you also need to surround yourself with people who have strengths in areas where you are weaker. An effective leader creates a culture where people willingly contribute and have confidence in their own decisions and ideas.

Anybody can lead a sheep. But why would you want to? I mean, as a leader it is just so much more gratifying to create leaders. It makes my day when somebody on my team comes to me with a plan. Maybe two years ago they might have been

★ ★ ★

39

coming to me with nothing but problems or timid questions, but now here they are, saying, "Here is what's going on, and here are five things I think we should do to make it better."

There are no words to describe how satisfying that is.

PLATOON SERGEANT TOP 5 TAKEAWAYS

1. Without leadership, nothing happens.
2. Leading by example isn't one way to lead—it's the only way.
3. Leaders create leaders and bring out the best in the people around them.
4. Anyone at any level can be a leader.
5. Leaders think things through. They have the self-discipline to remain calm and focused under pressure.

YOUR MARCHING ORDERS

If you are the boss: ask each person who works for you, "What do you value most about working here and what can I do to make sure you're able to give your best?"

If you are not the boss: find a process or system or task or marketing message that your company is using that just doesn't cut it. Think of at least three ways to make it better. Then, either bring your solutions to the boss or implement the best one on your own initiative.

★ ★ ★

B.B.B.
BEANS, BULLETS, AND BAND-AIDS

★ ★ ★

YOUR BUSINESS BATTLE PLAN AND BUDGET FOR STAYING ALIVE!

Your business must make a profit. NO EXCUSES!

Finances and budgeting are usually treated like a necessary evil, an afterthought better suited to bean-counters than warriors, but that's an attitude than can get a business killed. Your expenses must be lower than your revenue—NOW!—and you must work from a position of profitability. That means starting with a solid business battle plan that answers questions like: a) What exactly IS my business? b) Where do I want my business to be six months, one year, and five years from now? and c) What, specifically, will I do to get it there?

You don't have to be an accountant or bookkeeping professional to run a business, but you do have to know what's making you a profit and what isn't. That's why it's so critical to

★★★

make sure a budget—one you understand and will actually use!—is part of your business plan.

The budget is what holds you accountable to the plan. The budget is the reality check that keeps you and your business alive by keeping you aware of how much you are making vs. how much you are spending. We will be discussing how to take a completely different approach to what a budget is and how to use it as leverage in business. You must know where your numbers are at all times to win on the business battlefield.

BEANS, BULLETS, AND BAND-AIDS

"Beans, Bullets and Band-Aids" is military shorthand for minding the basics of preparedness. The initial steps in preparing for battle MUST include the means to provide the troops with food and water (beans), firearms and training (bullets), along with medical supplies and first aid skills (Band-Aids).

In the Marines, the Logistics Combat Element provides the supplies, services and communication that keep Marine Corps task forces ready for any mission. They coordinate the delivery and movement of resources, including people, weapons and supplies. The Logistics Combat Element is critical to Marine readiness and your budget and business battle plan are critical to running a successful business.

WHY YOU NEED A BUSINESS BATTLE PLAN

If you want to drive from Chicago to Albuquerque, do you just jump in a car, start driving, and see what happens? Drive real fast in no particular direction and *hope* you get there sooner or later? Not a chance. If you're a rational person you'll start with a roadmap or a GPS, and you'll probably check more than one to compare and consider your options. You'll ask people who have

★ ★ ★

made the drive before to give you advice. You'll find out how long it will take, what the landmarks and milestones are, which route suits your purposes best. You'll make sure your car is in good shape so it won't die on the way and leave you stuck in the middle of nowhere.

Then you'll customize your roadmap, marking the towns where you'll rest and refuel and the junctions to watch for, and the names and/or numbers of every road and highway you'll take. You'll print out that map and keep it right beside you for the entire trip, checking it often to make sure you're still heading in the right direction. Or you'll program your GPS with every important waypoint, and keep it in your field of vision at all times to check your progress and mileage.

Trying to run a business without a business plan is every bit as insane as trying to drive from Chicago to Albuquerque with no map, no directions, and no idea how to get there or how long it will take. In fact, running a business without a plan is even worse—it's like driving BLINDFOLDED! It will get you KILLED. But that's exactly what most business owners think they can get away with doing. And that's one of the main reasons they end up stuck. They run around in circles with no direction until they run out of time, money, and energy, risking burnout or even bankruptcy.

But YOU are not going to be one of them, because YOU are about to create a bullet-proof plan and a budget and keep them beside you on the seat the entire time you're at the wheel.

A business plan not only helps you stay on track, it also helps prepare you for battle. It becomes a kind of résumé and foundation for the entire business. It describes what the business really is, why you're doing it, who is on your team, your strengths and weaknesses, and most importantly—how much you intend to earn and what you will do to get it.

★ ★ ★

If your business model requires investment capital, you might already have a business plan you created to show potential investors. If so, ask yourself this question: is it a plan you actually use day-to-day or something you dreamed up to make the business look good on paper that you haven't looked at or thought about in the past six months?

If you think you don't need a plan because your business model is so simple, or because there's no need for investment capital at the moment—think again, soldier. Even if you were only driving from the house to the grocery store, doing it blindfolded would be suicide.

WRITING A BUSINESS BATTLE PLAN

Your business battle plan is one of the most important documents you will ever create as an entrepreneur. It will guide the direction of your company and also give potential investors a blueprint of the company's structure, commitments, daily operations, and future objectives.

There are entire books—LONG books—about how to write a business plan. Reading a few of them is a great way to educate you. But meanwhile, let's focus on the basics. What you really need here and now in the trenches is a simple plan that starts with where you are and what you've got and gives you a clear direction about what to do next.

The consultants and fancy graphics and appendices may or may not come later, but the kind of plan I'm talking about right here, right now, is one that covers the basics, one that you will understand and USE as a day-to-day action plan.

★ Start by writing a detailed description of the business and the nature of the product or service you are offering.
★ What is the purpose of the business and why does it exist? What drives the passion that made you start this

★ ★ ★

business? These answers will become your mission statement.

★ Make a list of competitors who offer the same product or service and point out how yours will be different and/or better. Dissect your competitors' strengths and weaknesses as compared to yours.

★ Who are your customers? How will they find you or how will you find them? This is the raw beginning of your marketing strategy.

★ What are your revenue goals per month? Per quarter? Per year?

★ What systems have you put in place to produce and deliver your product or service? To reach customers? To collect payment? To provide customer service and follow up? Think of all the steps in your process and the systems that will support them.

★ How will you track all your actions and results?

★ Write a 60-day action plan.

★ Write a daily action plan for the next seven days.

WHY YOU NEED A BUDGET

How do you know if a business is profitable? You measure it and check it often—weekly at least, because monthly is not often enough. And what you check is your budget. Once you've got a business plan, it's time to create a budget.

At its simplest, a budget is a way of knowing how much money is going out and how much is coming in so that you can make sure the latter exceeds the former. Just as the commander in tent needs to know exactly how to best use his supply of bullets, beans, and Band-Aids to accomplish his mission before his troops run out of ammo or starve to death or bleed to death, you need to know what your resources are at all times so you know how long you can hold out and how much risk you can afford to take.

★ ★ ★

And those resources include a business owner's most precious commodity—TIME. If you spend too much money, you can make more. If you lose too much money, you can find more. Money can be flushed. It comes and it goes. But time spent can never be recovered, ever. Tracking the time you spend—along with how much you are actually getting in return for that time— is one hell of an eye-opener.

Let's say a sole proprietors business grossed $16,200 last month. Pretty good, right? Not necessarily. If the month's expenses (taxes, rent, insurance, advertising, office supplies, postage, communications, and other miscellaneous overhead) came to $15,000, that means the net income is $1,200. If we divide $1,200 by the hours the owner put in, which at 50 hours/week times 4 weeks would be 200, we get the whopping rate of $6/hour. OUCH!

There are dozens of reasons to create and use a budget, but the top reason on the list is that a budget is an awesome motivator. You KNOW if you're only making $6/hour that something needs fixing or changing—not now, but RIGHT NOW. Whatever needs to happen, your budget is the reality check that shows you, loud and clear, that you need to do something differently. And revisiting your budget regularly will tell you if whatever you changed is working.

Maybe you start charging a realistic price for whatever it is you're selling, or setting a minimum fee that keeps you from wasting time on too many little, one-off deals. Or maybe you simply eliminate all non-essential expenses. The idea is to lead with revenue, not expenses. In other words, make money before you spend it.

On the other hand, you should be more concerned with the results you're getting from every investment than the amount of money you're spending. Does it make sense to hire someone at

★ ★ ★

$15 an hour when you're only making $6? Absolutely, if you are working on tasks and tactics that will grow the business instead of the kinds of tasks you can pay someone $15 an hour to do.

There's nothing like seeing those numbers start adding up in the win column. Still think budgets and plans are boring and unnecessary? Trust me, the thrill of watching your net income and your dollar per hour amount going up instead of down can be every bit as much of an adrenaline rush as closing a deal.

It bears repeating: your business MUST make a profit. Your business might have many noble purposes besides making money, but if it costs more to run than it makes in revenue, all those noble purposes will be out the window along with your business when it dies.

CREATING A BUDGET

It's not complicated to figure out and it doesn't take a math or accounting degree to understand, create, and follow a budget. And it's a great idea to do this yourself instead of hiring somebody to take care of it for you when you first start out. Why? Because that gives you a better handle on how the numbers work. You will KNOW what's going on instead of taking someone else's word for it. And—you'll be able to guide them in setting up the kind of reports that will make sense to YOU instead of having to read piles of printouts that confuse the hell out of you.

Tracking what goes out and what comes in grounds your business decisions and actions in reality. When you realize the true value of your time, you'll eventually recognize the value of hiring a bookkeeper or CPA. But there's no substitute for the self-education you'll get by learning to make and follow your own budget in the beginning.

Start with a simple Microsoft Excel spreadsheet—even do it with pencil and paper if you have to (You can also find a free

★ ★ ★

worksheet at: www.inthetrenchesbook.com/budget). Make rows for the months and columns for income and expenses. Fill in the blanks with everything you spent and made for the last six months. Based on your business plan, make projections for what you expect to spend and make for the next six months, making sure to have columns for:

1. Gross revenue—where your money is coming from.
2. Expenses—where your money is going.
3. Net Income—how much is left for you.

Take a look at what you have. The key is to make EVERY expense accountable for generating a measurable return. Figure out which expenses are essential and which are not, and cut the fat.

Hang your budget where you can see it and revisit it regularly. Schedule a weekly meeting with your team (even if your team consists of just you!) to review what's being spent relative to what return is being generated on each expense. The 30 minutes a week you spend reviewing your budget could save you thousands and keep your business from becoming a casualty!

When you and your entire team are committed and accountable to the business battle plan and the bottom line, your business will be turbo-powered instead of driving aimlessly. You'll be purring down a superhighway, eyes on the road, hands on the wheel, and with a world-class GPS keeping you pointed in the right direction.

GET EXPERT ADVICE

There's no need to go it all alone when there are so many resources out there to help with direction, structure, and accountability. As Warren Buffet once said, "Learn from

★ ★ ★

experience, and if not from experience, from those with experience."

When you've got a draft of your business battle plan and budget, show it to someone who knows more than you do, someone who's got a proven track record of business success. That could be a business coach, a mentor, a colleague, an advisor from your local Small Business Administration (SBA) office, a CPA, an attorney—you get the idea. Ask them to grill you on the details to make sure you haven't missed something obvious or set up unreasonable projections.

Ask them every question you can think of and LISTEN to their answers. Does that mean you have to take every piece of their advice as Gospel? Of course not. But it DOES mean that every idea and suggestion is worth considering seriously.

When you're through, make whatever changes need to made to your plan and ask them to meet with you again in two months, six weeks, whatever period of time will give you enough data to show whether you're making progress or not. Accountability is the name of the game. You could use your plans on your own and stay accountable to yourself, sure. But there's nothing like talking through your results and your reasoning out loud with a knowledgeable ally who will hold your feet to the fire—and who has the smarts to know how to help you put the fires out!

★ ★ ★

BBB TOP 5 TAKEAWAYS

1. Operating without a business battle plan is like driving without a map. Blindfolded.
2. Your business MUST make a profit.
3. A budget is essential for holding you accountable to your business plan and holding your business accountable for making a profit.
4. Track the time you invest as well as the dollars you invest—money can be made back but time once spent is GONE.
5. Stick with the basic needs to start with—bean, bullets, and Band-Aids. Luxuries can come later.

YOUR MARCHING ORDERS

Determine your ACTUAL hourly income for the past month.

HOW MUCH ARE YOU REALLY MAKING?	
Gross Business Income	
Business expenses	
Net business income (gross minus expenses)	
Hours worked	
Net income divided by hours worked	
Income per hour	

★ ★ ★

BONUS: BUSINESS BATTLE PLAN WORKSHEET

(For a free downloadable version of this worksheet, go to
www.inthetrenchesbook.com/battleplanworksheet/)

Summary and Description of the Business:

Business Commitments:
Year 1-
Year 2-
Year 3-

Business Owner Objectives for the Business:

Improvements YOU would like to make to the Business:

Mission Statement or Simple Idea:

Business Owner Needs and Values and DISC information:

Uniqueness of YOUR Business: (What makes YOU different
from the Competition?)

Marketing Plan: (Top 3 strategies)
1.
2.
3.

Tracking Your Marketing:

Systems Plan: (What things do YOU need to put in place to
make YOUR Business more effective and to work smarter
rather than harder?)

Revenue Goals: (per month or per quarter)

Daily Action Plan for the Business:

60-Day Immediate Action Plan:

★ ★ ★

EXPERT MARKSMANSHIP

★ ★ ★

HIT THE TARGET WITH EYEBALL-GRABBING, HEAD-TURNING MARKETING!

Be compelling! You might have the best operation, the best team, and the best systems, but if the phone doesn't ring, you won't get to use any of them.

A fancy marketing degree or an MBA is not required to successfully market and promote your business, nor does effective marketing have to cost big bucks. What you do need is a strategic approach to understanding your business, your goals, your customers, your competition—and then using that information to create a head-turning, eyeball-grabbing message. And remember the critical part that most entrepreneurs forget—track and measure the results of every tactic so you know exactly what's working and what isn't. Focus on lead generation, and market for tomorrow's business all the while you're servicing today's business.

READY, AIM, FIRE!

The Marines have a saying that, "Every Marine is a rifleman." No matter what your MOS, whether you're on the frontlines or in front of a computer, if you are a soldier you must learn to shoot accurately, responsibly, and confidently. You learn to choose, use, and care for your weapon. You learn to discipline your body and reflexes through relentless practice so that nothing disrupts your focus. You learn to identify and zero in on the exact target and shoot with precision to make every bullet count—because there are no second chances in battle.

Marine Corps Reference Publication (MCRP) 3-01B, Pistol Marksmanship opens by stating:

> Marines must have the versatility, flexibility, and skills to deal with any situation at any level of intensity across the entire range of military operations. Whenever the situation warrants the application of deadly force, a Marine must be able to deliver well-aimed shots to eliminate the threat. A Marine who is proficient in pistol marksmanship handles this challenge without escalating the level of violence or causing unnecessary collateral damage. It is not enough to simply provide Marines with the best available firearms; we must also ensure that their training prepares them to deliver accurate fire against the enemy under the most adverse conditions without hesitancy, fear, or uncertainty of action. To be combat ready, a Marine must be skilled in the tactics, techniques, and procedures of pistol marksmanship. (http://www.pointshooting.com/marine.pdf)

Marksmanship is a fact of life for every man and woman in military service. And marketing is a fact of life for every man and woman in business.

WHAT MARKETING REALLY IS

Marketing is attracting customers. Boiled down to its basics, marketing is all about getting noticed. You need to make sure the right people know how to find you, what you do, and why you're the best. It can be as elaborate as a slick ad agency branding campaign or as simple as flyers on windshields. The important

★ ★ ★

ingredient is the message: a reason for people to get in touch with you.

Marketing is not necessarily the same thing as advertising—advertising is just one of dozens of marketing tactics and plenty of those tactics are inexpensive or even free. It doesn't take a fortune to make marketing work, but it does take brains and creativity. Business owners sometimes tell me they're not doing any "marketing," but what they really mean is that they find ways to get the word out without having to pay for advertising. Even if all somebody ever does is put up business cards on bulletin boards at the grocery store, that's still marketing (whether it's effective marketing is another story).

We've all experienced the feast-or-famine roller coaster cycle of the freelancer, right? There's very little money coming in so you hustle like crazy to drum up business. Then you're slammed with projects and too busy doing the actual work to do any marketing. The projects get delivered and suddenly there's no money coming in so you hustle like crazy to drum up more business. That is a guaranteed recipe for BURNOUT. Riding that roller coaster can take all the fun—and much of the profit!—out of being in business.

Effective marketing is the kind that results in a steady stream of customers and revenue, and to get that result you need a system. The idea is to generate leads that fill your pipeline with prospects ready for conversion into customers.

- ★ **Lead:** someone who comes to you seeking your product or service. A lead may come in the form of a website visitor, phone call, or referral.
- ★ **Pipeline:** a pool of prospects who need your product or service and who are already interested in buying it from you
- ★ **Prospect:** a potential customer you're in contact with

★ ★ ★

★ **Conversion:** getting a prospect to the next step, whether it's a sale or an appointment or just getting them into your pipeline

The objective of a marketing system is to keep your pipeline so full that the next sale or the next project is always waiting in the wings.

IDENTIFY YOUR TARGET!

Remember that, "whenever the situation warrants the application of deadly force, a Marine must be able to deliver well-aimed shots." If you're under fire—or under imminent threat of fire—do you freak out and start shooting wildly in all directions *hoping* you'll get lucky and hit something? That's exactly what most business owners do with their marketing. When you ask them, "Who is your target audience? Who are you trying to reach?" they answer, "Everybody!" It happens so often there's even an industry term for it: the shotgun approach.

The ASSUMPTION is that the broader the target audience, the more potential customers you'll have. But the truth is the exact opposite. Trying to appeal to everyone means appealing to nobody.

And by now we all know that ASSUMING gets you KILLED and that TRY = FAIL! You cannot be all things to all people or you'll end up being invisible—you must be uniquely valuable to specific people.

The effective way to keep your pipeline full is to narrow down your target audience, not broaden it, and get very detailed about who your ideal customer is. Your marketing needs to be focused on the bull's eye, not the bales of hay surrounding it. And ironically, that focus will help you land people beyond the bull's eye, provided you have the time and doing so will not distract you from your focus.

★ ★ ★

Close your eyes and picture the perfect client for you. What do they wear? Where do they shop? Where do they live and why? How old are they? What keeps them up at night? What do they want more than anything on earth? Where do they get their news and information? And most importantly: what's in it for them if they buy your product or service?

Knowing as many details as possible is key to making all the right decisions about how, where, when, and how much to market to these people. If your target audience is 20-something computer programmers, are you going to reach them by buying a half-page ad in the Yellow Pages and sponsoring the next AARP luncheon? Definitely not!

It's not so much about data and demographics as it is about REAL PEOPLE. A perfect example is a remodeler I know who is now always busy. He's got a waiting list of customers and even has to turn down work. When I asked him who his target audience was, he said, "You know, it's that couple who have been married for at least 15 years. You see them at every home show. They come in holding hands and you can tell they're happy with each other and they know what they want to do next with their house. That's my target audience. A few other customers I work for are outside that scope, but more than 80% of them are right in there."

I asked him why he thought that was. "They're married for the long haul and there's no question that they're gonna stay together. They're ready for a change but don't want to move because they like their house. And they have the money to spend to do it right because there are two incomes."

★ ★ ★

MARKSMANSHIP EXERCISE #1

★ Describe your Ideal Client/Customer in detail.
★ What is their motivation for doing what they do?
★ What is their #1 problem or burning desire (which relates to what you offer)?
★ How does your product or service satisfy that need?

Knowing your target audience inside and out is the starting point that dictates every marketing step you take: your message, your delivery, your tactics, your timing, and your budget. If you're unsure exactly what your audience is looking for—ask! Interview as many people as possible who fit your target audience and find out. Make sure you're listening to what they want and the language they use to describe it and use that same language when YOU describe it.

YOUR UNIQUE VALUE PROPOSITION

What value do your customers get from your product or service? And why should they buy from you instead of the competition? Answer both of those questions clearly and simply and you've got a unique value proposition.

MARKSMANSHIP EXERCISE #2

★ Write a paragraph about yourself, your product, or your business/service.
★ Describe the strengths of what you offer.
★ What is the #1 benefit your Ideal Clients/Customers get from what you offer?
★ What do your Ideal Clients/Customers get from what you offer that they can't get anywhere else?
★ How is what you offer different from and/or better than the competition?

★ ★ ★

Specificity counts! Remember, trying to be everything to everybody gets you lost in the sauce like a meatball. Specialists are ALWAYS more valuable than generalists, and it's better to be known as THE expert in a well-defined niche than someone who does a little bit of everything. Whether it's true or not, the common perception is that "jack of all trades, master of none" is worthless!

Your unique value proposition must be based on what's in it for your audience. If you spend a fortune to broadcast to the world, "I'm the best!" or "XYZ Company is the industry leader!" What does that mean and who cares? Will that make me pick up the phone and call you? Hell, no!

"We sell houses," is not a value proposition. "We work exclusively with pre-qualified buyers so we'll sell your house faster for a higher price," is getting closer. Outdoor retailer REI could say, "We sell quality recreation products." So what? So do dozens of other retailers. But REI's value proposition is that everything they sell is 100% guaranteed, period. No matter when you bought it or how heavily used it is, they'll take it back if you're not happy. If I'm about to invest $300+ in a new pair of mountaineering boots, where do you think I'll buy them? That's right, someplace where I can be sure I won't end up screwed and out $300 bucks if they don't work for me.

Specificity has other advantages besides keeping things simple and compelling to your target audience—it helps you keep your focus on what you do best.

Here's an example of how that focus works. At Zuber Group, a specialized real estate team, our target market is residential homebuyers and sellers in Eagle, Idaho at a $300,000 price point. We market to them specifically, but we still get calls from outside that market. When that happens we have the option to refer them to other real estate professionals. As a result, Zuber

★ ★ ★

Group stays focused and keeps from getting pulled in five different directions.

We make the commitment to set boundaries because we know we can service this product and these people correctly. Going too far outside those boundaries would jeopardize the integrity of the business. Honoring these boundaries means my team continues to get better and better at our specialty, and it builds our reputation for integrity at the same time.

TELL THEM A STORY

Marketing is more than just benefits and taglines and bullet lists. You also need to make an emotional connection with people, especially if your product or service is abstract—or expensive! People make decisions for logical reasons, yes, but mostly we all make decisions based on our gut reactions and first impressions. The likeability factor has a lot more influence on every business transaction than anyone usually admits.

A story helps people understand how your product or service relates to them and to their lives. It helps create a picture in their minds, so they can see themselves moving forward to take that next step in your process. There are all kinds of stories. Case studies are examples of how your product or service benefited someone just like them. A story about how you got into the business and why you LOVE what you do can also be the clincher that wins their heart and gets their business. The best stories are easy to remember and compelling enough that your customers will pass them on and tell them even when you're not around.

LOCKED & LOADED: YOUR MESSAGE IS YOUR BULLET

Have you ever watched a Super Bowl ad that was knock-your-socks-off spectacular, and then had absolutely no idea what the product was? That's because the message was missing. One of

★ ★ ★

the biggest mistakes business people make is hiring somebody to design the coolest logo or the flashiest website so that it looks absolutely great—but says NOTHING. The prettiest flyer on planet Earth will not generate one dime's worth of ROI unless it communicates a MESSAGE. Your audience must be able to instantly grasp what you offer, why they should care, and what they need to do next.

1. And that message is made up of three elements:
2. Your unique value proposition
3. Your compelling story
4. A call to action

That last bullet is overlooked way too often. Tell people what you want them to do when they get your message. Do you want them to call for an appointment? Fill out an entry form? Visit your website to claim a free offer? Then tell them. DO NOT ASSUME THEY WILL FIGURE IT OUT. Make it easy on them. Every piece of collateral you put out there needs to have a clear call to action: your website, your flyers, your voice mail greeting, your email signature—everything.

Write to sell! Get to the point right away. Take headlines, for example. If the headline doesn't grab their attention, they'll never read the rest. That's why the header is more important than the body text, even though it's critical to get them both right. It might take two hours to put together one paragraph and a bullet list, but it could take twice that or more to figure out exactly which five words need to go in the headline or the subject line. You only get one chance to make a first impression, so make it count and take the time. And if you're not good at words and writing, hire someone who is or ask for help!

Look at your product or service as if you were the customer. What features and benefits would you care about? What would make the difference between buying and just thinking about it?

★ ★ ★

OFFER SOMETHING FREE

It's Sunday morning, you're flipping through all 12 pounds of the Sunday newspaper and all of a sudden you get the ads and the next thing you know, you and the kids are at R.C. Willey buying something you didn't need. Why? Go back to the ads. Was it the living room set on sale? The words? The photos? Or was it the free frickin' hot dogs that got you into the store?

Everyone should offer something FREE. Everybody!

While you're honing in on the exact words to capture your message, remember that it must be believable. Make sure you are crystal clear on your strengths. You must be in an excellent position to deliver value to your customers. If YOU believe in what you're doing, that comes across. Modern day audiences see through bullshit and they know hype when they see it. If you're going to convince anyone that your product or service is a great value, then you better freaking believe in it and believe in yourself! If you have any doubts about how good you are—then get better, RIGHT NOW!

When you project confidence, you instill confidence in others. They know it. They can feel your excitement.

★ ★ ★

TOP FIVE TIPS FOR CREATING AN EYEBALL-GRABBING, HEAD-TURNING MESSAGE

1. Stress the benefits—instead of telling them what your product does, explain what they will enjoy as a result of what it does. It's all about THEM, not about you or your business.
2. K.I.S.S. Keep it short and simple.
3. Offer something FREE.
4. Keep it real. No hype, no exaggeration, no making shit up. Your audience is way too smart for that.
5. Make ample use of these hot-button words: FREE, GUARANTEE, YOU, MONEY, UNBELIEVEABLE, AMAZING, INTRODUCING, WOW, UNIQUE, AT LAST, NEW, WHY, NOW, SAVE, VALUABLE, TODAY, HOW TO, HOT.

POP A FLARE: BRANDING

In the trenches, when it's time to get extracted—to get the hell out of there or die—and you've got to make absolutely sure they can find you. That's when you pop a flare, and it better be so bright and unmistakable that the right people know EXACTLY who and where you are.

Without that flare, you're dead. You're lost in the sauce. In the business trenches, popping a flare will save your life. And in marketing, the flare that gets you noticed and keeps you memorable to your customers is your brand.

Branding is more than a logo or a tagline—it's the overall image that supports and conveys your message. It makes you easy to find, easy to remember, and easy to understand.

For branding to work, everything about that image needs to be consistent. Think of Willie Nelson. What do you picture—an old Martin guitar with a big hole in it? Long braids? A bandanna

★ ★ ★

headband? That's Willie's brand; he positioned himself as an "outlaw" bucking the country music establishment more than 30 years ago and he has stayed in character ever since. Have you ever seen a video or photo of Willie in a polo shirt or a tux? Why not? Here's a guy who could afford a decent haircut and a tailor and the latest top-of-the-line model Gibson or Martin makes. But the only guitar he ever plays—in public at least—is the old beater. That's branding consistency.

Once you've defined your target audience, your unique value proposition, and your message, you need an overall look and feel that reinforces all three. That's where your logo, your colors, and your style come in. That's when it's time to pick an image and stick with it.

Your message may change slightly over time, in fact it will probably have to if you want to stay ahead of the curve and continue meeting the needs of your ideal clients/customers. But your brand shouldn't change. The look stays the same. Huge corporations like Coca-Cola or Nike can afford costly "rebranding" campaigns, but rebranding successfully takes tremendous amounts of exposure and cash.

Branding goes beyond your marketing materials. Make sure that everything your target audience experiences about you is consistent with your message, right down to how you dress, how you talk, the causes you support, and whether you close your emails with "Sincerely," or "Later."

CHOOSE YOUR WEAPONS: MARKETING TACTICS

So—do you need a website? An ad agency? A toll-free number? Which marketing tactics should you use? The answer depends on who you want to reach and what impression you want to project. There are dozens of marketing tactics, and many of them are

★ ★ ★

inexpensive or even free. It doesn't matter which tactics you use—what really matters is choosing your tactics for solid reasons and knowing how to make the most of what they can do for you.

Take websites, for example. Everybody thinks they've got to have a website, but just having one is not enough. If it just sits there without a regular infusion of new content or a plan for attracting visitors, it's worthless!

To make the most of a website, you have to think of it as part of a chain and make sure it does its part to keep that chain from breaking. If you're running an ad that promises a free gift to anybody who visits your website, make sure the URL link in the ad goes DIRECTLY to a landing page that talks about the free gift and helps them get it right now. If you let them end up on your home page and make them do detective work to figure out where the free gift offer is hiding—you will frustrate them and lose them.

Or let's take blogs. They need care and feeding. If you launch a blog, make sure you've got a plan for feeding it with fresh content on a regular basis and promoting it by networking with other bloggers.

In real estate, signage is key for visibility. A sign is a very powerful tool because it's right there in the yard of the house being offered on a highly trafficked street for great exposure. Anyone driving by sees the realtor's number and can call right then, right there. But you need to think about context, too. If your sign sits in the same yard for six months, what message does that send? It tells the world you have great exposure but ZERO results.

Your tactics also need to be appropriate for your brand, your target audience and your industry. Yard signs are very appropriate for realtors. Yard signs would be a bad idea for say, a marriage counselor.

★ ★ ★

And make sure that no matter which tactics you're using, everything is branded with your logo and includes complete contact information.

Here's a list of the most common marketing tactics:

- ★ Business cards and stationery
- ★ Websites
- ★ Blogs and Ezine Articles
- ★ Social Media (Facebook, LinkedIn, Twitter, etc.)
- ★ Newsletters
- ★ Direct mail
- ★ News releases
- ★ Email
- ★ Pay Per Click
- ★ Craigslist
- ★ YouTube
- ★ Event sponsorships
- ★ Networking
- ★ Billboards
- ★ Classified ads
- ★ Television and radio spots
- ★ Brochures
- ★ E-books
- ★ Coupons
- ★ Presentations and demos

TAKE CAREFUL AIM: PLANNING AND STRATEGY

I said earlier that effective marketing requires a system. So not only are we going to spend every shot wisely, we are also going to track where every bullet landed so that we'll know how to aim better next time.

★ ★ ★

The system starts with the budget and the business plan. Make marketing investments you can afford and track the results to find out what your return on those investments is. Always ask new leads how they heard about you. And build your systems by working backward from your desired outcome.

Here's what that might look like. Let's say your target objective is $200,000 in revenue and your average transaction is $5,000. That means that you need 40 transactions in order to make $200,000. If your ratio of leads (calls coming in) to closed transactions is 10:1, then you'll need 400 leads to get to 40 transactions.

Now let's look at where your leads will come from if your top two marketing tactics are yard signs and direct mail. Break each one down. How much does it cost you per sign? What's the average number of calls per sign you get? And how many of those calls result in transactions? If signs cost $50 each, and each sign only gets you an average of two leads, how many signs will you need to produce 400 leads? And how much time do you need to invest putting up signs, following up, and creating the messages on those signs?

Direct mail is a great example, because off the top of your head you probably think it's a real long shot. Let's say you have a direct mail piece with a great message, a FREE offer, and an urgent call to action, but your ratio of direct mail pieces to closed transactions is 500:1. Pretty dismal, right? Not necessarily. If each direct mail piece costs $1 with a ratio like that, you will make $5,000 by spending only $500.

I am NOT suggesting that everybody should start using direct mail. These are just examples to show you how to systematically determine which tactics are the most productive and most cost-effective.

★ ★ ★

The only way to know that is to track EVERYTHING you do, everything you spend, and all of your results. Ask everyone who contacts you how they heard about you. Dedicate unique phone lines for incoming calls so that you'll know which ones are coming in response to which ads. Track where your website visitors are coming from.

★ ★ ★

EXPERT MARKSMANSHIP TOP 5 TAKEAWAYS

1. Know your target audience, specifically and in detail.
2. It's not how good your marketing materials look; it's how powerful your MESSAGE is.
3. Marketing is an ongoing system—work your plan to keep your pipeline full.
4. Be unique and be COMPELLING!
5. Track everything; number of leads, number of closings from those leads, results from all marketing tactics, and dollars spent per lead.

YOUR MARCHING ORDERS

Interested in learning how YOU can launch a MONEY-MAKING venture without investing a dime of starter capital? It's easy!

Go to: www.inthetrenchesbook.com/cabostory/ right now and download the FREE e-book, "No Money. No Problem!"

See how this works?

★ ★ ★

5 X 5 LIMA CHARLEY

★ ★ ★

LOUD AND CLEAR COMMUNICATION!

One of the best ways to win others over is with your ears—
by listening to them.

In battle conditions, signal strength and clarity are rated on a scale of 1 – 5. "5 x 5 Lima Charley" is the code for "I understand you perfectly—loud and clear." This chapter is about the extreme importance of being clear; listening first, validating everything, and assuming nothing. It's about keeping your message short, compelling and precise.

It's about the vital importance of making sure your clients are completely understood and everyone is on the same page. Ask questions. Without clarity and understanding there will be assumptions, and the minute that you assume anything in business or in battle – you're dead!

LOUD AND CLEAR!

In the Marines, as in every branch of the Military, communication must be loud and clear. The word "loud" does not literally mean shouting all the time (even though it usually does!); it means making sure the message gets heard, especially

★★★

when M249 SAW machine guns, M16 assault rifles, and M203 grenade launchers are firing all around you!

That urgency doesn't change, even during a lull. Just because it's downtime right now doesn't mean IEDs aren't about to start exploding again at any second. Even in the calm before the storm, sending and receiving have to be done with crystal clarity because if you're going back to the trenches, you've only got time for a few words.

So that message better be very simple and very clear and very loud and your team better know exactly what they're supposed to do. I mean, if those orders take more than ten seconds to deliver or people don't understand exactly what you mean, they're dead. Their lives are on the line.

That's where "5 x 5 Lima Charley" comes from—it's a shorthand code that serves as VALIDATION. The signal strength of the transmission is 5 on a scale of 1 -5: I can hear you. It's loud enough. The clarity of the transmission is a 5 on a scale of 1 – 5: I can understand you. There's no static or interference. "Loud and clear" means I understand you perfectly and know exactly what to do next.

That kind of language needs to be learned by heart—that's a big part of what boot camp is for. There is relentless training so that you have a specific language of a few carefully chosen words that CANNOT be misinterpreted. For example, A is always alpha. And it's alpha because there's no time for back and forth about, "Did you say A or was that I?" or risk of confusion because of different accents. We all know alpha is the letter "A."

★ ★ ★

ALPHABET CODE LETTERS FOR 5 X 5 LOUD AND CLEAR			
A	Alpha	N	November
B	Bravo	O	Oscar
C	Charley	P	Papa
D	Delta	Q	Quebec
E	Echo	R	Romeo
F	Foxtrot	S	Sierra
G	Golf	T	Tango
H	Hotel	U	Uniform
I	India	V	Victor
J	Juliet	W	Whiskey
K	Kilo	X	X-Ray
L	Lima	Y	Yankee
M	Mike	Z	Zulu

A.L.L. OR NOTHING!

Communication goes much deeper than telling people what you want them to know. It's not about interrupting to get your point across or broadcasting an uninterrupted stream of information. On the business battlefield, communication means LISTENING.

True communication goes both ways. It is not a one-way barrage. If you want to be heard, start by making a real effort to understand what the other person is telling you, whether they're saying it in words or nods or stony silence. Why? Because unless they trust you and believe that you care about their side of the story, they will tune you out no matter what you say or how you deliver it.

In every business interaction, the formula for real communication is: A.L.L. or nothing—Ask, Listen, and Learn.

★ ★ ★

Ask questions for clarity and listen to the answers instead of assuming you've heard them right.

If you say to me, "I'll meet you at six o'clock." Is that a.m. or p.m.? If you don't specify and I don't ask, how will we know? I mean, I could *assume* you must mean p.m. because I'm rarely up at six o'clock in the morning, but whose fault is it if one of us doesn't show up for the meeting? We're both responsible, and we both suffer the inconvenience of not having that meeting. And all it would have taken to clear everything up was five seconds to ask one simple question. The true professional makes sure there is 100% complete understanding before walking away or hanging up.

So, in rethinking communication, we're establishing that it's not about telling people what you think they need to know or do. It's about finding out what they want. It's about listening.

VALIDATE EVERYTHING—ASSUMPTIONS WILL GET YOU KILLED!

Validating is a fancy word that basically means reassurance. It's simple and it works like this: you say something to me. I believe I know what you mean, but just to be sure, I ask a question to confirm that I've heard you correctly.

Validation is an incredibly powerful skill. Why? Because it establishes trust, courtesy, and respect. When you take the trouble to ask clarifying questions and repeat back what they just said, to make sure you got it right, people realize you're actually listening to them. It establishes the foundation for the entire relationship.

And—validating everything you hear guarantees that you are paying attention and not missing anything important. When most people are in a conversation, they spend the entire time the other person is talking formulating what they're going to say in

★ ★ ★

reply. We all do it; we're all guilty of it at some point. But, if you know you have to confirm what you've just heard and repeat the gist of it back to them out loud, you know you have to listen.

Remember the Golden Rule? "Do unto others as you would have them do unto you?" Forget about it! Find out how they want to be treated and give them what THEY'RE looking for, not what YOU ASSUME they're looking for.

Awhile back I made breakfast for my kids. I went all out and made pancakes, thinking I was giving them this great treat and they'd love the surprise and think I was the world's best dad. By the time they got to the table, each one had a plate all dished up with pancakes, butter, and syrup. That's how everybody eats pancakes, right? Wrong.

My daughter took one look at her plate and started crying. She only wanted butter. Instead of making her day, I made her feel like nobody cared about what she wanted. It's mind blowing, the kind of life-changing information you can get just by asking instead of assuming.

Validation continues even after the transaction is over. Ask for your clients' feedback with surveys or emails or a phone call. Following up shows that you're still listening, even after you've finished the job. It's crazy that more business people don't bother to do this, because it makes a huge positive impression on customers. And that's not the only payoff—it also gives you priceless feedback on how to make your product or service BETTER. Ask them what you did well and what you could do better next time.

The idea is to create a relationship where they're excited to talk to you when you do call to follow up with them. Because they know you listened to them, and more importantly that you CARE. That's what it all boils down to. This person cares. He's not just out to make a sale.

★ ★ ★

To find out what your clients or prospects or customers want, ask them. Just ask. And when they tell you, ask another question or two to make sure you heard them right. It's that easy.

BUSINESS BATTLEFIELD CLARIFYING QUESTIONS

★ Can you tell me more about that?
★ What didn't you like about that?
★ What do you mean by that?
★ Sounds like _____ is really important to you.
★ Can you help me understand that a little better?
★ How come?
★ When you say _____, what does that mean to you?
★ Could you explain that to me in more detail?
★ Why is that a concern?

WARM UP THE CROWD

No professional speaker starts a speech by launching right into a complex subject. Walking straight into a meeting and starting to make the pitch before anyone even sits down is a classic mistake too many business people make. A business conversation is rarely (if ever!) all business. Small talk is a big deal, because it gives all parties a chance to relax and get a feel for each other as people. And the best way to loosen anybody up is to get them talking about themselves.

Stop thinking about the end result you're looking for from this meeting and learn something about them. As a realtor, when I meet with people, they all know what I do, so I don't even have to bring up what I do. So I start conversations about them. How? By asking about their family, their occupation, their recreation, or their dreams. It's called F.O.R.D.

F.O.R.D. – **F**amily, **O**ccupation, **R**ecreation, **D**reams

★ ★ ★

We talk about their family. I ask how their career is going, whether the economy has had an impact on them. If that doesn't get much response I'll go to recreation. "Do much skiing this year?" "Catching any fish these days?" "How about those Cowboys/Steelers/Broncos, etc.?" Or move on to dreams. "When was the last time you took a vacation? If you could go anywhere in the world, where would it be? Really? Why?"

It's simple compassion. Succeeding in business means genuinely caring about the people you do business with. That does NOT mean you have to be best friends with every client or call them up and invite them to your house every weekend. It just means you take the time to settle in and focus. Tell a joke. Talk about the weather. Engage your listener by opening up with something other than your message to see how they respond. Ask them if they're winning these days. You'll get all the clues you need to read their reactions and shape your style and delivery to match what fits their personality.

The funny thing about using this getting-to-know-you approach is that the conversation always leads back around to business and to what I do—but it happens on their terms, when they start asking me about the market or about whether interest rates are up or down. That way, they never feel rushed or pushed. And because I'm not rushing them, everything goes smoother and faster.

A friend of mine is in the process of buying a car. She's smart, successful, and single. And frustrated. "It happens every time," she tells me. "I walk into the dealership and everyone who works there assumes that I'm shopping on behalf of a husband I don't have." End result? She gets fed up and leaves. NO SALE. Assumptions like that will get you KILLED.

★ ★ ★

FIVE STEPS TO OPEN ANY BUSINESS CONVERSATION

★ Ask FORD Questions that generate positive energy and open dialog.
★ Listen carefully to your clients needs so you can establish value.
★ Ask more questions to help each other get clear.
★ Validate what you've heard to gain trust and understanding that you care about what they are saying.
★ Set expectations for the entire process.

SETTING EXPECTATIONS AT THE OUTSET

We all feel more comfortable in situations where we know what to expect and we know what's expected of us. One of the best ways to put your clients or customers at ease is to explain how this is all going to work for them and what it will look and feel like.

In a meeting format, make sure to have an agenda and to go over it together before getting started. It can be simple and verbal, or it can be a printed outline; the format isn't important. What matters is creating understanding about what you're going to do and discuss. It establishes a time frame, and it helps keep you on track. It also helps introduce and transition into the business reason for the meeting.

But an agenda does more than that—it also gives you a way to show them they can count on you to do what you say you're going to do. In laying out what's about to happen, you're making promises. We'll start with this. We'll move on to this. We'll end on time at whatever o'clock. When you make sure that all of that

★ ★ ★

happens in a way that keeps all those promises, you establish credibility.

Another key step is to educate them about YOUR PROCESS so they know what to expect from you. For example, if your system is to typically call all your clients every Friday or send email updates twice a week, let them know that so that they know what to expect and they don't misunderstand and think that you're bugging them or that you're desperate. Everybody says that there's no such thing as too much communication—but unless your give your contacts a heads-up about what to expect, you could unintentionally send the wrong message.

So, to draw the line between over-communication that is a good thing and over-communication that is just plain annoying, get it straight in advance.

STUDY PERSONALITY PROFILES

It isn't necessary to be a psychologist to be in business. But if you're going to sell anything—and remember, if you're not selling you are not in business—you'll get much better results by educating yourself about personality profiles. There are many different assessment tools out there; Meyers-Briggs, DISC, Discover Your Strengths, it's a long list. What they all have in common is that they help you understand how to adjust your communication style to get along better with a number of different personalities. The objective is to understand it enough to get a reading on who that person is across the table.

This works in all aspects of life. I'm a direct person. Big surprise, right? My wife on the other hand is more social and emotional. When we have a conversation, I tend to be passionate and intense and direct, with no intention of intimidating her. But on her side, on the receiving end, that can come across as me

★ ★ ★

yelling at her. The fact that we know this about each other helps prevent the kind of misinterpretation that could escalate into some serious marital discord!

That's why you have to understand whom you're talking to and adjust accordingly. Tailor your message and your delivery style to the personality profile of the person you're with. With a direct person, get right to the point. If you launch into your pitch and talk for the next 15 minutes, they will cut your head off. They're not interested. "Just give me the bottom line. Cut to the chase. Not now, but RIGHT NOW." What's it going to cost me? How long is it going to take? That's what a direct person wants.

Emotional people will be concerned with what's going to happen with the entire process and how it's going to affect them during the transaction and whether they'll be taken care of after the project is complete. They want to know all of those things.

Then there are the detail people. If you're dealing with an analytical person, you better be prepared to go over that contract line by line because they will insist on getting everything 100% clear and every question answered before moving forward. The good news there is that everything gets clarified. But the risk with analytical people is that they sometimes over-think the situation to the point of talking themselves right out of the sale.

How do you know which personality profile you've got in front of you? Watch for nonverbal cues! If you're speaking and they're not nodding or saying yes, and they're shifting their body in their seat, something's off and you better switch directions quickly. And if what they're saying doesn't match their body language, it's time to switch tactics. Always trust the nonverbal signals over the actual words somebody is saying if the two aren't matching up.

For example, if I'm speaking to you in a direct manner and you're not a direct person, I will be able to tell something is off.

★ ★ ★

You'll shift, you'll fidget, and you'll show signs of being uncomfortable that I need to recognize in order to pull in the reins or shift gears or go in a different direction.

PERSONALITY PROFILES – ONE EXAMPLE

The tool my team uses is the DISC personality profile system. It is a detailed assessment provided by a trained administrator, but for now, here is the layman's summary to help you understand how DISC works.

D = Driver Style = Conviction!

I = Expressive Style = Flair!

S = Amiable Style = Warmth!

C = Analytic Style = Accuracy!

With the natural differences among the four behavioral types in mind, pretend that you have asked four people to work together to make three simple decisions in 15 minutes:

1. Where the next meeting will take place
2. When the meeting will take place
3. The theme of the meeting

Your group consists of one Amiable Style, one Analytical Style, one Driver Style, and one Expressive Style who all believe in practicing The Golden Rule, that is, "treat others the way you would like to be treated." Do you think they'll get the job done? Let's see why this may not work out.

★ As they walk into the room, the Driver typically speaks first. "Here's my plan…"
★ The Expressive says, "Hey! Who died and left you boss?"

★ ★ ★

★ The Analytical says, "You know there seems to be more here than meets the eye. We might want to consider some other relevant issues and break into sub-committees to explore them."

★ The Amiable smiles and says, "We may not get this done if we don't work as a team like we have before."

Now consider another scenario. Let's give four people of the same behavioral type the same assignment. They'd get the job done, wouldn't they? Not if they follow the Golden Rule!

★ What do you call it when you send four Driver Styles into the same room? War!

★ Or four Analytical Styles? Paralysis by analysis!

★ And four Amiable Styles? Nothing! They sit around smiling at each other: "You go first." "No, why don't you go first. By the way, how's the family?"

★ When four Expressive Styles walk out, ask them if they've gotten the job done. "Get what done?" They've had a party and instead come out with ten new jokes and stories.

Obviously, I am exaggerating to make the point, but not by much. Driver Styles tend to have the assertiveness and leadership initiative to get tasks started. They may then delegate to others for follow-through, enabling the Driver Styles to start other new projects that interest them more.

Analytical Styles typically are motivated by their planning and organizational tendencies. If you want a task done precisely, find an Analytical Style. Of the four types, they're the most motivated to be correct; they're the quality control experts.

Amiable Styles have persistence and people-to-people strengths like patience, follow-through, and responsiveness. When we have a problem, we may choose to go to a sympathetic

★ ★ ★

Amiable Style because he or she listens, empathizes, and validates our feelings.

Expressive Styles are natural entertainers who thrive on involvement with people. They also love to start things, but often do not finish them. In fact, they may pick up three balls; throw them in the air, and yell, "Catch!" Emotional, enthusiastic, optimistic, and friendly, Expressive Styles usually pep up an otherwise dull environment.

COMMUNICATION TECHNOLOGY

In the 21st century we've got a zillion ways to send and exchange information—email, voice mail, Facebook, Twitter, texting, Skype, NetMeeting, Blackberry's, MySpace, iPhones, smart phones, laptops—and most people in business are connected almost 24/7. We've got email and landlines and cell phones and social media and even good old snail mail: the USPS.

One of the biggest challenges with all this technology is figuring out who uses what, and how, and when. That's why one of the most critical questions you need to ask, as early as possible in every new business relationship is, "What's the best way to get in touch with you? Texting? Phone? Email? Twitter DMs?" Get 100% clear about their top three, in THEIR order of preference. Then make absolutely sure that information is in your database and part of your system for staying in touch with your contacts.

Some people won't leave voice mail messages because they assume you have caller ID and will see that they've called. These same people are often the ones who assume everybody else is doing the same thing—so they never listen to their voice mail messages, figuring they'll just call you back when they get a chance.

Some write everything that's on their mind in long, detailed emails. If they're on a Blackberry you'll get short, abrupt notes

★ ★ ★

with no signature. Or, they might have three different email accounts and they rarely check the one they gave you. Some people use texting and Twitter direct messaging (DM) exclusively and only check their email every few days. Some have email alerts turned on 24/7.

And don't forget about faxes—yes, the fax machine is a dinosaur, but it's not extinct yet and if your best client likes faxes better than emails, you'd better be sending that client faxes and not emails.

The big three tools in my business are still meetings, phone calls, and email, in that order. An in-person conversation is absolutely the BEST means of communication because it gives you a ton of nonverbal information about what's happening as it happens. You get instantaneous feedback from the person you're communicating with and can adapt on the fly if something's not working. You get to earn trust and confidence by using a firm handshake and direct eye contact. As you're speaking, you can tell in less than a second whether the person you're with is glazing over or getting it—by the expression on their face, or a sudden tensing up, or a big open grin, or a million other signals happening all the time in every conversation.

A telephone conversation is still live and in real time, but you lose the opportunity to communicate visually, through body language. You can still read between the lines by paying attention to someone's tone of voice, or those sudden long pauses—but it's more difficult and takes more focus. The advantages of a phone call over email are that it gives you a chance to make a human connection and use that personal touch. You're giving someone your time and the sound of your voice and laughing at their jokes. Secondly, it's live, so one five-minute phone conversation by phone can settle something simple that could take half a dozen back and forth emails.

★ ★ ★

That brings us to email. The pros: it's fast, you can say what you need to and move on to do something else, whatever you've said is on writing for C.Y.O.A. purposes, and whoever's on the receiving end can read it at their convenience without getting interrupted by a phone call.

But there are great big cons. Email just never gives you all of the answers. Unless you and everyone else is correctly anticipating every possible question that could be asked back, the odds are there will be something missing and more back and forth will be needed to clarify. And email is so easy to misinterpret. Without those voice cues that let somebody know if you're kidding, a little joke might get taken as a big insult.

The biggest problem with email is that everybody has their own different protocol about how to use it. How many times do you reply just to say, "OK?" How do you know if the recipient opened your email yet? You ASK! If you need a response, ask for a response. And if there's no response after you've asked for one, call them up and make sure they got it. Make sure it didn't get stuck in their spam filter. That one phone call might take 30 seconds and save you from losing a customer.

In these times, to stay in touch with clients, prospects, and everyone you work with or interact with on and off the business battlefield, you better be locked and loaded with an arsenal of communication devices and skilled at using all of them, because your people need to be able to reach you when they need you, not now, but RIGHT NOW. And when they need to hear back from you, it needs to be TODAY, not whenever you get around to it.

K.I.S.S.

So what goes along with being wired and connected 24/7 so that we all get with Blackberry's, smart phones, texting, headsets, and on and on and on? You got it. An avalanche of information that

★ ★ ★

takes time to weed through to decide what's important and what is not. Your clients' time is precious—and YOUR time is precious—too precious to waste.

Follow the K.I.S.S. principle: Keep It Short and Simple (also known as Keep It Simple, Stupid!). Get to the point. Your prospects and customers do NOT want long, drawn out spiels— they want to know the parts of the message that are important to them, in plain English. Clear, concise, short, and simple.

Your communication is only effective when you present it in a language your audience understands. Do not—DO NOT— make people work to connect the dots. Understand their educational level and their demographics and communicate to them accordingly.

The trick is to make it as easy and convenient as possible for them to do business with you. If they're looking confused, simplify it even more or use a story or analogy. And when you know they've got it—STOP TALKING.

TAKE THE TIME TO MAKE IT CLEAR

Picture this. You sent your assistant an email about a task you wanted him to take care of, but it wasn't clear. Something was left out or lost in translation. Happens all the time. He didn't understand and therefore did not act on it. You're frustrated because you didn't get the outcome you needed, which makes you look bad to the client. Your assistant is frustrated because he takes pride in his work and now he feels responsible for the screw up, even though it wasn't his fault. Everybody looks bad, everybody is frustrated.

The worst part of this sad story is that it would have been so easy to avoid the problem in the first place. Taking one minute— even 30 seconds—to validate and ensure clarity can save 30 days' worth of disaster cleanup later.

★ ★ ★

Have you heard that saying, "When there's not time to do it right, there's always time to do it over?" Take that time. Ask, do you understand? Is this what you mean? Could we go over that once more so that I'm clear on what you need?

Take the time to listen to your voice mail and let people finish their sentences before you butt in to interrupt. When you get an email—READ THE ENTIRE EMAIL. If you're too ADD to do that, then get an assistant who will do it for you, but make sure you have a system in place to ensure that nothing gets missed or ignored, or you'll pay later and pay dearly.

Thank your clients for the time taken to listen and respond! No matter what the outcome of your communication, even if the response to your talk or discussion has been negative, it is good manners to end it politely and with respect for everyone's input and time.

★ ★ ★

5 x 5 LIMA CHARLEY TOP 5 TAKEAWAYS

1. The #1 objective of effective communication is mutual UNDERSTANDING.
2. One-way communication is no communication at all. Listen first, speak second.
3. Validate everything! Always ask to confirm that you heard correctly.
4. Learn to adjust your message and delivery to different personality styles.
5. Always do what you say you're going to do—ALWAYS! NO EXCUSES.

YOUR MARCHING ORDERS

How do you come across to others? How does your personality and communication style affect every business interaction? It's time to find out. Go to www.inthetrenchesbook.com/profiles/ and take the free personality assessment.

★ ★ ★

S.O.P.
STANDARD OPERATING PROCEDURE

★ ★ ★

QUALITY SYSTEMS
SAVE YOUR BACON!

Without systems, your business is chaos and confusion.

The creation and ongoing use of systems and Standard Operating Procedures (SOP) are not optional for a soldier or a business owner, they are 100% mandatory. Running a tight ship is a matter of precision and drills to hone your skills until perfect execution becomes habitual and automatic.

This chapter shows you how to break your business down into categories, define the results you need in each one, and then create and implement systems for achieving and tracking those results—no excuses! You'll learn to use technology as a tool to work smarter instead of harder by making these drills the backbone of your day-to-day operations.

★ ★ ★

WHAT EXACTLY IS A SYSTEM?

Technically speaking, a business system is a working combination of people and procedures, supported by technology, organized to meet a specific set of business objectives. Put more simply, a system is a methodical, repeatable way to make sure the right things happen, consistently and efficiently and on time.

To stay alive, you must be able to create new business and maintain existing business. And that is what systems and technology were invented for.

EXAMPLES OF SYSTEMS

Systems can be very simple. When you walk into your house, do you put your keys in the same designated place, every time? That's a system. Using it means you always know where your keys are without having to waste any time or energy even thinking about it, let alone searching frantically to find them when you need them.

Or take a lawn sprinkler system, for example. Instead of having to remember to water the lawn manually and make sure each section gets watered in the right volume at the right times, a homeowner who has a sprinkler system gets to enjoy their lawn and garden without ever having to worry about watering it—even when they're away on vacation.

In Real Estate we use automated programs and applications such as Top Producer, iContact, Settlement Room, and iCalendar or Microsoft Outlook for calendar reminders. We have lead generation systems for making that phone ring! And systems for what to do after it rings and prospects are entered into the contact management system.

A system can be something as simple as using a program to track all your pending and completed to-do items, ensuring

★ ★ ★

nothing gets overlooked. Or a system can be as complex as an automated program for contact management that enables your team to touch base with your clients on a daily, weekly or monthly basis—all without any mental effort from you!

Systems make sure that things get done and done right, instead of falling through the cracks.

SYSTEMS ARE 100% MANDATORY

Think you don't need systems? Better think again. The business battlefield is one hell of a competitive environment. Winning demands precision. Just winging it DOES NOT CUT IT anymore. With the right systems in place, your business will operate smoothly, with the least possible effort and energy expended. Your business will be more profitable and much easier to run. Systems are the key to delivering a consistent, repeatable, excellent performance.

Establishing systems ensures that every part of your business is being used to its full potential.

If you are buried in the trenches, taking the time to develop necessary systems to help support you and leverage your time will ensure a positive outcome in the end. The odds are it may not be instantly gratifying; however, there will be immediate impact!

Every aspect of your business needs a system, to gauge productivity, effectiveness, and GROWTH!

Here are just a few of the priceless benefits of creating and using business systems:

★ Systems create organization and streamline operations.
★ Systems give you direction and accountability.

★ ★ ★
93

★ Systems make you look more professional and your product/service more valuable.

★ Systems organize and automate daily tasks for consistency and efficiency.

★ Systems improve your level of customer service and hence, customer satisfaction.

★ Systems make you and your team more productive and more efficient.

★ Systems free up your time and energy for bigger and better purposes.

★ Systems help you stay on top of what's working and what isn't.

★ Systems will increase your price per hour.

And there's more. If you ever decide to sell, the fact that you've got working, documented systems will GREATLY increase the value of your business.

DIFFERENT KINDS OF BUSINESS SYSTEMS	
System	Benefits of Using It
Restaurant Point of Sale system	Speeds up workflow, tracks which items sell best, provides staff performance information
Time management system	Keep appointments, meet deadlines, track tasks
Content management system	Makes sure entire team has the most current version of any document
PC file backup system	Ensures that no critical files are lost
Lead generation system	Creates a list of potential customers
Flow chart	Process follows each step in the correct order to reach the desired result
Organizational chart	Everybody knows who is responsible for what and who reports to whom

★ ★ ★

CONSEQUENCES OF NOT HAVING SYSTEMS

Without systems, your business cannot grow. Period.

For many entrepreneurs, creating and maintaining systems sounds b-o-r-i-n-g. They like the heroic stuff, not the detail stuff. Systems are all ABOUT repetition and being methodical, and there are lots of creative, dynamic individuals out there who think they're way above doing detail work like that.

Here's the reality: if you're trying to operate a business without creating and maintaining systems, not only is your business headed for fatality, you're also making everything you do harder than it needs to be. Instead of growing, flowing, and succeeding, you'll be digging yourself deeper and deeper into chaos, confusion, and burnout.

Here are just a few of the consequences of NOT using systems in your business:

- ★ Burnout
- ★ Frustration
- ★ Loss of credibility
- ★ Damage to important relationships
- ★ Lost opportunities
- ★ Stagnation
- ★ Loss of TIME

Think you're too busy to bother with systems? Then I ask you this: busy doing WHAT? If you are attracting plenty of business, but are not able to maintain that business, I can pretty much guarantee that most of whatever you're doing with your time is not making you any money. Never forget that there is a big difference between "busy" and "profitable."

★ ★ ★

HOW TO CREATE YOUR BUSINESS SYSTEMS

It's brain-dead obvious that systems are necessary, and they can be very basic. Creating a system is simply the act of making and using a plan for a specified outcome. You'll need action systems—to make sure things get done—and information systems—to track every action, every investment, and every outcome. You start with what, when, where, who, how, and why.

★ What happens after you receive a call from a prospect?
★ When will you follow up or communicate with them next?
★ Where will you meet? Where will you deliver any information they need beforehand?
★ Who will make sure it gets delivered?
★ How will it be delivered—in person, via email, by fax, by phone?

Why does this need to happen, what is the desired outcome (in this scenario, the desired outcome might be to build a relationship or convert the prospect into a client)?

In the Military, we call it the Rules of Engagement.

R.O.E. – RULES OF ENGAGEMENT

★ When military force may be used.
★ Where military force may be used.
★ Against whom force should be used in the circumstances described above.
★ How military force should be used to achieve the desired outcome.

To begin, break down your business into categories. What functions make up your business (for example: sales, marketing, lead generation, product delivery, etc.)? Think of every aspect

★ ★ ★

and write it down. Then take a further look at each category and specify its purpose. Why do you need to do that in your business? What does that function accomplish?

Next, specify your objectives for each category of your business. What do you want to get? What results would you need to consider this aspect of the business successful?

By answering each of the above questions, you'll get a clear picture of your desired outcome. Next, work backwards from that outcome to trace what you need to do to get there, step by step. Note what has to be completed and when, and then WRITE IT ALL DOWN.

Congratulations—you now have a procedures manual.

Start keeping track of what you do, how, when, and how long it takes. What steps are taking too much of your time? Where are you having problems? Think about how you could do things differently, step by step, and decide how you'll track what changed.

Systems design all goes back to a needs basis. What is missing? What keeps falling through the cracks, and why? What are we not doing that we should be doing?

Once you've taken a thorough and brutally realistic look at questions like these and made a list of answers, you're ready to start developing systems that work.

Here's an example of a system my team uses every day:

★ ★ ★

ZUBER GROUP—NEW PROPERTY LISTING SYSTEM

Listing Appointment: Email listing appointment checklist to Team Coordinator

★ Team Coordinator will prepare Comparative Market Analysis (CMA) for agent and pre-selling packet.

★ Agent is responsible to email Team Coordinator with comparable properties

★ Team Coordinator will email listing prospect the pre-selling packet, tax records and CMA or can print them for delivery.

★ Team Coordinator will email listing prospect a copy of the seller marketing plan email.

★ CMA/Seller Packet-cut and placed into company folder.

★ ★ ★

NEW LISTING

Upon submission of fully signed listing paperwork and listing checklist Team Coordinator will complete the following items:
★ Create listing file to be kept in office for agent's review
★ Verify all paperwork is complete and confirm that high resolution photos were submitted
★ Enter listing in MLS
★ Enter listing in Top Producer database
★ Add to Client for Life –Contact Management program
★ Email full detail listing to agent for proofing
★ Create virtual tour
★ Create YouTube video
★ Enter listing on all websites and post ads (Including Postlets, Blogs, Social Media)
★ Prepare in-home binder for listing
★ Provide agent with yard sign
★ Provide agent with lockbox and enter in Supra to track showings
★ Make introduction call to sellers when listing is live
★ Create flyers
★ Email listing details to entire team along with YouTube to post on Agents Social Media Sites
★ Email the sellers with seller marketing email containing all marketing links
★ Mail sellers the team listing letters-series of 6 letters over listing period
★ Check Supra every morning and email agent with any showing feedback
★ Once a week email seller with update and feedback info, also check on flyer status etc.

AGENT RESPONSIBLITIES FOR LISTING:
★ All listing paperwork
★ High resolution pictures
★ Completed Listing Checklist-submitted with listing paperwork
★ Delivery of sign, lockbox, binder and flyers
★ Agent makes follow up call to client once a week

NEW LISTING DEADLINES:
★ Listing must be submitted by 10 am to have everything done that day.

★ ★ ★

BRING IN THE REINFORCEMENTS!

Believe it or not, there are human beings out there who actually enjoy creating and maintaining systems and who are brilliant at making them work in ways that make you more money. If you are a business owner, one of the smartest moves you will ever make is to hire one of them.

There are two kinds of people in this world: creators and maintainers, and I am definitely a creator. Like a lot of other entrepreneurs, systems aren't especially exciting for me, and at first I thought I could get away without any. I soon learned otherwise. After I got my ass kicked over and over by losing business because I would forget to call people back or I would let something fall through the cracks, I finally realized I needed help and hired my world-class assistant, Amanda.

It was the scariest step I had taken up till then. I was going to have to PAY somebody on a regular basis, whether or not I SOLD anything! I was terrified. Did it turn out to be a major pain in the ass to bring her up to speed on what I needed and to work through figuring out what was broken and how we could work together to fix it? It was excruciating. Did everything change overnight? Nope.

And was it worth it? HELL YES!

Within four months, everything flipped. With Amanda's expert support, the business turned around and took off to a whole new level. The return on investment for her salary was amazing in bottom-line terms, and priceless in sanity terms. Knowing that all the critical details I hated worrying about were being taken care of gave me the confidence to perform at the top of my game. The lesson? Hire TALENT. Talented people will push you to get answers and get results, continually raising the bar for the rest of the team.

★ ★ ★

Now that we had systems to keep me accountable and a super-competent person to use and maintain those systems – I could focus on what I do best: SELLING! Instead of standing by the fax machine for three hours a day.

If you need support to make your systems work, GET IT. Get creative and think of a way to afford it; like paying them on a per-transaction basis to get started. Or see how you like working with a part-time virtual assistant. Make the time to train them and to communicate LOUD & CLEAR about what needs to happen and when and what it should look like when it succeeds. Give them the guidance they need to operate autonomously, show appreciation, and celebrate victories together.

CHECKLIST FOR HIRING THE BEST

1. Check as many references as possible.
2. Have them take a personality profile test.
3. Conduct multiple interviews about specific topics.
4. Test them with questions about what they would do in certain circumstances.
5. Bring them on temporarily at first to ensure a great fit.

SYSTEMS TECHNOLOGY

Technology – cell phones, PDAs, smart phones, laptops, wireless connections, and so on – allow you to be extremely efficient. Portable tools like these mean you can take advantage of "found time" between appointments and tasks, wherever you happen to be. That means you can eliminate a lot of down time.

Another point about technology is that it has totally changed people's expectations. In today's world, your customers and potential customers have less patience than ever. Receiving and delivering information quickly is vital to success. Respond right away to their questions, or your business will soon be DEAD!

★ ★ ★

Every day, new software programs come out that help busy professionals get things done and keep track of everything that happens in their business. Do a Google search on "time tracking" and see all the hits you get that feature everything from programs you can buy to free downloads to web-based programs that take up no space on your hard drive. It's all out there, and it's worth your time to research which tools will work best for your business needs and your working style.

If cost is an issue, look for bargains. There are web-based contact database management programs out there for as little as $10 per month. There has never been a time in history when business systems have been as cost effective as they are now.

Once you choose a program, invest the time in administrative set up and customizing the features. And make sure a specified individual is personally responsible for every system—technology WILL NOT WORK without an OPERATOR.

Automation is a beautiful thing. Let's say you implement an automated contact management system. You set it up to communicate effectively so that all you have to do is hit send. Your clients see regular contact efforts coming from you and you stay fresh in their minds because of that. By making sure the emails are sent during regular business hours (as opposed to 3:00 am), you give the impression that you're sending them personally (as opposed to automatically). You are still there for them. From your clients' perspective, it makes it look like you are always on top of your game.

And that perception is PRICELESS.

★ ★ ★

SYSTEMS ONLY WORK IF YOU USE THEM

Your systems won't get you out of the business trenches unless you USE them. That means making DISCIPLINE and COMMITMENT daily, mandatory habits.

How many business owners do we all know who have QuickBooks installed on their office PCs—and they never get around to using it? Is your mileage log up to date? Is your business set up to run smoothly, even when you're not there? Because if it's not, you are DEAD!

When you're under fire, the fact is you'll forget something. You need support, and that's what the system is for. If you're in the trenches and you're about to get annihilated, your systems—combined with the discipline and commitment to use them—will give you the step-by-step direction that keeps you in action.

Look at it this way. Your business is like a car. And a car is, in essence, a system. Maybe you bought it brand new, but it still needs to be maintained, it has to be serviced, it has to be evaluated on a regular basis. Your business works the same way. Time goes by fast and nothing is static in this life. At least monthly—preferably weekly—make time to sit down and take a cold, hard look at what is working or not and what you will systematically do RIGHT NOW to make it start working better.

THE DRILL INSTILLS DISCIPLINE

Marine training always includes the drill. The objective is to "drill" discipline into new recruits by pummeling them harder the more they resist, until they break and accept the fact that getting good at drill will keep them alive. Until they reach that point of breaking, recruits will resist the training. They may

★ ★ ★

think they're good enough, they may reject the need to do drill or they may reject the commands.

The objective is to break that individual down in order to build him or her back up again, much stronger and more focused than before. Creating and implementing business systems means dissecting your business down to its smallest pieces to determine what really counts. And then putting those pieces back together so that everything you do has a purpose and a focus and is aimed toward achieving a clear result.

Athletes and soldiers have incredible control over their bodies. How do they develop that? It comes from practice, training, discipline, and commitment. For most people, strain, stress, laziness, fear, and discomfort get in the way of peak performance. When situations become stressful, dangerous, or uncomfortable, those who have been trained to make their bodies conform to their will undoubtedly perform better than those people whose only mind-body training has been computer games or casual sports.

A Marine recruit will spend what seems like an eternity standing motionless at attention, sometimes in unbearably cold or hot weather. But with each such session, the cold becomes a little more bearable, the motionlessness becomes more familiar and more elegant and the recruit's body learns a little better how to conform completely to the wishes of its operator.

In a tactical situation, on sentry, you must remain completely quiet and motionless in order to minimize the chances of being seen or heard. A recruit who has mastered hundreds of hours of drill, in the cold and in uncomfortable positions, will also be a master of his own body in such tactical situations.

When a recruit moves on to skill at arms training, the habit of calmness, despite discomfort, is an essential ingredient to making a good shot. If a recruit is not used to ignoring the minor

★ ★ ★

discomforts of a held position, their minds will be distracted and their firing will be less accurate.

Once the drill is internalized and your body is accustomed to the discipline, it becomes more like a relaxing meditation than hard work, and your mind becomes free. Once a business has working systems that have become a daily habit, the beauty of that drill is that no matter what hits the fan, no matter what disaster strikes, that business will stay on course. Even when IEDs are exploding, your systems will ensure the best possible performance and the best possible results.

★ ★ ★

S.O.P. TOP 5 TAKEAWAYS

1. The creation and ongoing use of systems are mandatory for running a business.
2. Systems will increase your price per hour.
3. Without systems, your business cannot grow. Period.
4. If you need support to make your systems work, get it. Hire TALENT!
5. Systems only work if you use them, with discipline and consistency.

YOUR MARCHING ORDERS

Are your systems working? Here's one way to find out. Take an entire day to turn off the world outside. No calls, no email, no pets, no kids, no TV—pretend you're taking your business into a bomb shelter for a time out. Do this within the next seven days, no excuses!

Look at everything that's been going on for the past six months. It all boils down to two questions:

★ What is happening?
★ What is not happening?

Where are you having problems in your business? What is the weakest part of your business? What is most time consuming? What are you struggling with? Look at the parts of your business that you feel do not run as smoothly as they could.

What steps will you take to fix it? How will you change your systems to change your results?

★ ★ ★

And don't forget the good news. What did you do that worked well? How can you create or adjust a system to help make it easier to do it more consistently and predictably?

★ ★ ★

S.O.R.T.
SPECIAL OPERATIONS & RESPONSE TEAMS

★ ★ ★

TENACIOUS NEGOTIATION!

If you can't go around it, over it, or through it,
you had better negotiate with it.
– Ashleigh Brilliant

In business, you only get what you're willing to negotiate for. Negotiation is an inescapable part of being in business and whether you realize it or not, you're doing it all the time. When you hire a contractor or work out a delivery date you're negotiating. When you finally have that come-to-Jesus talk with the client who never pays on time, you are definitely negotiating. And if you've been putting off that talk, it's probably because you're afraid of losing a customer or being outmaneuvered—or of hearing the word, "no."

Negotiation happens every day. Every day, all the time, regardless of what kind of business you're in. The only way to get want you want is to ask for it. There are even ways of asking that will have the other party convinced that whatever you're asking for is their idea, not yours.

★★★

Truly great negotiators are skilled at protecting and advancing their best interests AND making both sides come out of it feeling better off than they were. Like chess masters, they're always thinking several moves ahead and when they inevitably win, they do it respectfully and tactfully. And you, my friend, are about to become one of them.

WHAT IS NEGOTIATION?

It's easy to get negotiation and closing confused, and they do have many aspects in common. But boiled down to the barest bones, the main objective in closing is advancing a long-term relationship. The main objective in negotiation is WINNING. Yes, win-win outcomes are always the ideal to aim for, but when that's not possible it's time to get tenacious about coming out ahead.

It comes down to determining in advance what winning looks like to you in this particular situation. What do you really want and need to get out of this? More money? Better terms? Future business? If your objective is to get more practice so you can become a better negotiator, then you win just by showing up and diving in, no matter what the outcome is. Ask for something extra that wasn't already part of the deal. And remember—making the other side feel like they've won is a form of winning, too.

At its simplest, negotiation is the fine art of asking for what you want and getting it. Without a show of force.

DIPLOMACY: SPECIAL OPERATIONS AND RESPONSE TEAMS

War is a hell of a lot more complex than seeing who's got the superior firepower or the most troops or even the most guts. All of those elements matter—HELL yes! But what happens before war is declared and after it's over—when the terms of surrender need to be worked out—is just as critical as what happens on the

★ ★ ★

battlefield. History is full of examples of conquerors who won the war but lost the peace. Why? Because they knew how to fight, but they did not know how to negotiate.

Even in the heat of battle there are critical turning points where victory means saving lives instead of taking them. Take a hostage situation, for example. When it's time to rescue civilian hostages it's time for big brains, not big guns. That's when Special Operations and Response Teams (SORT) are called in.

To successfully handle a hostage situation you have to be 100% ready for ANYTHING. When you're a SORT commander you definitely need to be locked and loaded and fully prepared to use whatever force might be necessary—and cool-headed enough not to resort to using it rashly. You must have the territory mapped out in your mind down to the smallest detail. You need to get your hands on every single piece of intelligence about who your opponents are, who the hostages are, what's motivating them, how much food and water and ammo they've got, what their weak points are—anything and everything you can use as leverage.

And most importantly—you need to have the skill and experience and laser-sharp focus to walk that thin red line; to make exactly the right moves at the right times, for however many hours or days or weeks it takes, when the wrong move could get everybody killed in mere seconds.

When you're dealing with an adrenaline-crazed terrorist whose gun is aimed directly at an innocent hostage's head, you'd better be one f***ing brilliant negotiator.

GO IN SMILING, NOT SWINGING

The critical skills in negotiation are being tenacious and keeping your cool. Always remember that tenacious does NOT have to mean confrontational. Nobody likes to be backed into a corner.

★ ★ ★

Therefore, raising your voice, and being forceful, or making threats may work against you in the business trenches.

Your objective is to get somebody to do something for you or sell you something at your price on your terms. So you want to avoid making them defensive or suspicious. No matter how eager they are to close a deal, nobody wants to do business with an asshole. Instead, make it easy for them to say yes. Make them feel like your objective is their idea. You do that by paying attention, by listening. And you do it by taking your ego completely out of the equation and staying focused on the issues, while recognizing that both sides may have strong emotions about the process and the outcome.

Always treat the other party with respect, even when they're being unreasonable—ESPECIALLY when they're being unreasonable. And speaking of unreasonable, make sure that what you're asking for is realistic, respectful, and supported by facts you're prepared to present calmly and clearly. Making a ridiculously low offer that you doubt will fly can be counterproductive.

Keep your cool and kill them with kindness. If the other party senses hostility on your part, they'll withdraw and you'll lose the opportunity to gain critical information from a comfortable discussion. He who keeps control of his emotions keeps control of the negotiating process. And the same goes for the party who does more listening than talking.

Sometimes one word can give away a hidden agenda. Or a fleeting change of facial expression will reveal their true position. Dig in with probing questions—then shut up and listen! Often, they will slip up and give you more information than they meant to. Generally speaking, the more you can get the OTHER party to talk, the more you will learn about their stated position and their true wants and needs behind that position.

★ ★ ★

Armed with everything you learn by listening, you're then in a position to negotiate from their point of view—using their own arguments as leverage to show how agreeing to YOUR plan will help them get what they want. The best approach is, "How can we work this out so we both get what we want?

Bottom line: Negotiating honestly and respectfully builds trust. Demonstrations of aggression erode it.

HONESTY TRUMPS TRICKERY, ALWAYS

It may come as a surprise to learn that there is no substitute for truthfulness and honesty in negotiating a business transaction. Bending the truth, providing inaccurate information or even outright lying to get your way is sure to backfire sooner or later. If the other party loses confidence in your credibility during negotiations, the deal may not occur. If the other party experiences surprises following the closing of a transaction in which inaccurate information was tendered, your business is dead. On the other hand, truth and honesty, even when it hurts, will win the trust and confidence of the other party (both during and after negotiations) and will give you more credibility and a stronger position in future negotiations.

DRAW YOUR LINE IN THE SAND

The first step in negotiating anything is between you and yourself, not you and anybody else. Define what winning looks like to you. Because if you go into a negotiation without a clear picture of what you want to accomplish, how will you know if you've won or not?

Figure out what you've absolutely got to have first, and then prioritize the other points you're willing to be flexible about. Every businessperson must learn to draw their own hard line in the sand and stick to it. What's your walk-away point? What are you willing to lose this deal for? I mean REALLY lose it for?

★ ★ ★

Let's say you're in the market for a late-90's Honda Accord with less than 100,000 miles on it that has never been in an accident and your budget is $4,500. You find one that's been meticulously cared for by a single owner who saved all the maintenance and repair records and is happy to show them to you. It's got 79,000 miles on it, not a single dent or ding, and has just had the timing belt, brakes, and tires replaced. Its market value is $8,900. The seller won't budge below $4,900. Are you prepared to walk away from that deal without any regrets? If the answer is "Hell, no! Who'd walk away from a sweet deal like that?" then your REAL number is $4,900, not $4,500. That's what I mean by defining what you're willing to lose the deal for.

There's more to making a deal than price. What are the ironclad policies of your business that are not negotiable, no exceptions? Maybe you insist on a written estimate and a signed contract before you send payment. Or you charge a minimum fee for every project. Or work on any new project doesn't start until the deposit is paid.

If your true walk-away number for hiring a graphic designer to create a new brochure is $1,000 and you find one you'd love to work with but her minimum fee is $1,250—it's time to say no. If you are a graphic designer whose minimum fee is $1,250 and a potential client offers you $1,000, it's time to say no. You have to decide where to draw the line between letting a deal go and letting yourself down.

You are in business to make a profit, and if crossing your own line undermines your profit margin then LET THIS ONE GO. If you cross your own line, you're changing your business model and pricing structure for somebody you probably don't even want to be working with. Your time is valuable. Your product or service is valuable. Your time is priceless. Clients who are more concerned with price than quality usually turn out to be the clients who are the biggest pain in the ass. Nothing is ever good enough for

★ ★ ★

them. And because you already let them get away with screwing you once, they'll keep trying to do it over and over again.

That's why you draw your line. It isn't worth changing your business model or sell yourself short for anybody. I don't care if it's your family, your friends, or the freaking Pope—the minute you are doing business differently than your business model, your business is DEAD! You just opened Pandora's Box.

NEGOTIATING STRATEGIES

★ Attack: fight them into a corner and dominate
★ Appease: make sure everybody's happy; cooperate and compromise
★ Analyze: solve the problem with logic
★ Flee or Evade: withdraw, threaten to walk, or withhold communication as a tactic

GET REAL NUMBERS ON THE TABLE!

If you really want to cut the fat and start getting somewhere in a negotiation—get the other party to give you a number. Find out as early as possible in the process whether it's worth your time to even negotiate. Most people resist doing this. They're afraid that if they disclose what their budget really is too soon, they'll be giving away some kind of advantage. But until you've got realistic numbers to deal with, everybody is just dancing around in circles playing chicken. To go back to the car example; once I know that you want $4,900 for it and I want to spend $4,500 we can finally start negotiating.

In most cases, working out how to bridge the gap between a price you're willing to accept and what I'm willing to spend is the easy part. The hard part is getting those numbers out! There is this myth that if you give somebody your bottom line, they're going to go right for it; that if you tell them your budget is $500,

★ ★ ★

they will charge you $500 even if their usual price is $250. That is bullshit.

How many times have you spent hours on the phone in multiple calls with a prospect talking about everything BUT price because you were afraid to bring it up and scare them away? And then you finally do throw out a number only to find out their budget is nowhere near your ballpark and never will be? How did it feel to have wasted all that time, for nothing?

Every business deal has to have a strong element of trust. Whether you're the client or the vendor, at some point for anything to happen you need to see the other side as a professional, as a business partner, instead of an enemy who's out to screw you unless you watch them every minute.

To negotiate effectively instead of going in circles that go nowhere, establish a starting point. Name a price.

THE Q-TIP PRINCIPLE = QUIT TAKING IT PERSONALLY!

Eliminate ego and emotion from the equation and stay focused on the issues. Ask yourself:

What's best for my clients?

What's best for my business?

What does the other party REALLY want/need out of this and how can I demonstrate that my plan will be a win for them?

★ ★ ★

BUSINESS BATTLEFIELD NEGOTIATION TACTICS

Pre-Negotiation

★ Get locked and loaded by arming yourself with facts, documents, and convincing reasons why it's in their best interest to move in your direction.

★ Know everything you can about the process and the details of time, money, pitfalls, what's happening in the market, etc.

★ Find leverage points you can use.

★ Draw your own line in the sand—define what will make this a win for you as well as what points you're willing to be flexible about.

★ If possible, study personality profiles in advance to decide how to present your arguments.

★ Prepare alternatives and options to present in case your Plan A doesn't fly.

During Negotiation

★ Instead of rushing to make the first demand—LISTEN very carefully to the other party's interests first.

★ LISTEN to what is and is not being said. Read the nonverbal signs for clues about what the other party really wants and needs.

★ Ask questions to confirm what you're hearing and prevent assumptions and misunderstandings.

★ Establish some parameters to set a businesslike tone and context for discussion. What are the possibilities? The alternatives? The boundaries? The consequences of not reaching an agreement?

★ Get real numbers on the table.

★ Find out who makes the decisions in each party. Who has what power in the relationship? Who stands to lose the most if an agreement isn't reached?

★ ★ ★

★ Determine if time is of the essence to them—and if it isn't, find a way to make it so!
★ Brainstorm ideas about various alternatives. Think outside the trench and be creative!

PUT IT ON PAPER!

Talk can be cheap, so the best negotiating tactic is often "put it on paper" meaning, write it up! Or in other words, show me the money! When you put it on paper and show people the money it can change the entire dynamics of a situation. They know you are serious and that makes them more likely to move forward.

Troubleshooting

★ When you're negotiating with difficult people, avoid responding to provocations. Instead, ask them how their solutions will solve the problem.
★ If the other party is stonewalling and won't budge, ask straight out, "What will it take for you to move forward?"
★ Take the risk out of it for them. Offer a guarantee. Commit to doing the work over if they're not satisfied with it the first time.
★ If all else fails, see what happens if you take it away from them. I'm not suggesting that you get all pissy and storm out. What I'm talking about is more like, "We don't seem to be getting any closer on this. What's your gut feeling at this point—is this going to work or should we stop wasting each other's time?"

★ ★ ★

Ending the Negotiation

★ Make sure everyone's responsibilities are clearly spelled out.

★ Document what you've agreed to, whether in a formal contract, a letter of agreement, or even something as simple as an e-mail that all parties reply to with their OK.

★ Make sure to include a sense-of-urgency element—this means all parties have a time-based incentive to implement the agreement and negative consequences for not following through.

IT DOES NOT HURT TO ASK

Most people are much better negotiators than they think. You may not remember it, but you were an expert negotiator when you were a kid. You were creative and very effective when it came to negotiating candy, cookies or toys. My son Zac and my daughter Aspen are some of the best negotiators on the planet. Not only that, but they have the power to negotiate without money, power or authority. They're either describing me as the best dad ever, giving me hugs and kisses and the sweetest looks (using their melt-dad's-heart tactics) or they're kicking and screaming and crying (using their tantrum tactics).

And they are PERSISTENT. They keep up the pressure until they prevail. If you want to see what real tenacity looks like, come over to our house around bedtime. Every night I've got to renegotiate the details of getting ready for bed and they'll push the envelope wherever they see the tiniest opening. Who's going to read the story? For how long? Can we stay up five minutes later? Why not?

At three and six years old, they're relentless. Both of them. Every single night. It's war.

★ ★ ★

Little kids have basically two tactics: they engage in behavior they know you can't stand so you'll give in to make them stop. Or they butter you up and pour on the sweetness until you give in to make them keep it up. It works because they know your weaknesses.

But what they've got going for them more than anything else is this: they are not afraid to ask and they will not take "no" as a final answer.

Business is about making a profit, yes, but in negotiating there are many, many other factors that have to be negotiated. There's time, level of detail, quality, guarantees, quantity discounts, extra service, means of delivery—the list is practically endless.

If you want to get good at negotiating—start practicing. Start bargaining. Just ask. So many business people I work with are so afraid to hear the word "no." But if you start asking, you'll be amazed how often you'll get a "yes!" See past the risk and go for it.

I have a friend who travels a lot. And she always gets the best room in every hotel she stays in, without paying extra, because she asks for it. She walks in, finds out which room they've given her, and politely but unrelentingly asks for a better one until she ends up with the one she wants. "Usually, the first room they give you is one they want you to settle for. And most people do," she says.

"But for me, it's not really about the room—it's the idea. My goal is to get the best room in every hotel, every time, paying the standard rate. It has become a game for me and now I look forward to it." Not only that, but playing this "game" on a regular basis keeps her at the top of her game in terms of her negotiating skills.

★ ★ ★

Like my kids, my friend knows the value of not being afraid to ask. She once called Royal Caribbean and asked them to hold 110 spots for client's friends and family. "I was all prepared to do some tough bargaining, and they said "okay." Just like that! I couldn't believe it."

I love to ask for discounts or extras or some off-the-wall thing—just to see what happens. I do it in a friendly, joking way. I even ask for discounts at the grocery store—and sometimes it works!

Maybe it's because nobody else does this that I take them by surprise. I make it fun for them, too. I'll say something like, "Come on, man! This apple—look at this thing. Ninety-eight cents? Are you serious?" and they laugh and say, "All right, you can have it for...oh, heck, you can just have it."

The best way to get really good at negotiating is to practice in situations that aren't life or death. When you've got nothing to lose, what harm is it there in asking? And if asking scares you, is it because you're scared they'll say no—or are you really scared they'll say yes?

★ ★ ★

S.O.R.T. TOP 5 TAKEAWAYS

1. In business you only get what you negotiate for.
2. Go in smiling, not swinging—be tenacious but keep your cool.
3. Get locked and loaded—arm yourself with supporting facts, relevant documentation, and anything else that will give you leverage and help you come up with alternatives.
4. Draw your line in the sand and honor it.
5. Tenacity is key! If you want something badly enough, you'll do whatever it takes, for as long as it takes, to get it.

YOUR MARCHING ORDERS

Get out there and negotiate something that has nothing to do with your business. Ask for an upgrade on your next rental car. Go into the quick-lube shop and ask, "So what kind of a discount are you guys going to give me today?" with a big smile. When they seat you at a restaurant, ask if there's any possibility of getting a better table.

The next time you make a purchase—any purchase—ask, "Is that your best price? Would you throw in [*name something extra*]?" Then watch what happens.

★ ★ ★

ADAPT AND OVERCOME

★ ★ ★

THINK ON YOUR FEET AND SWITCH TACTICS!

*You must take personal ownership of looking ahead
and staying alert to keep your business alive!*

It's an ever-changing business world; you MUST be able to adapt your strategies and tactics to stay ahead of opposing forces or your business is dead. You must do more—and do it better—with less in order to get your business through economic downturns. The trick is to evaluate the situation, decide what to keep and what to cut, and then hang tough until the Business Battlefield Law of Equilibrium reasserts itself. Then, it's opportunity time! Change is never easy and major change can be painfully difficult. However, long-term success requires it. SO GET USED TO IT! This chapter shows you how to get great at it.

HANGING TOUGH

In business, everything starts with a plan. The plan provides a map, a direction, and the basis for well-thought out systems for getting where you're going. What a plan does best is give you a way to proactively take responsibility for every possible factor

★★★

within your control. But business is still part of life on Earth, where things don't always go according to plan. Customer's needs change. Markets shift. New competitors show up. Shit happens.

So what do you do then? Pack it in, close up shop, sit down and cry, go back to bed, head to the nearest bar? Do you GIVE UP? Hell no. It's just LIFE and changes and surprises are all part of the game, so you pick yourself up and take a good look around and get creative about new tactics and a better strategy for winning. THEN you act.

The worst mistake people make in the trenches is getting that sequence backwards—they want to react first before taking time to think it through. As in, "Shoot first, ask questions later." And that's what gets them in trouble.

Let's say a landscaping business is suddenly losing long-term customers. They think "Oh, no! We better start advertising, right away!" And so they start shelling out big bucks for radio and TV spots and full-color newspaper ads. Pretty soon they're not only out of customers, they're also out of money, and maybe even on the verge of going out of business.

When crisis strikes, the first step is always to stop and think. Before doing anything, remember to remain calm. Create a strategy. Come up with a new Plan A. In some cases, you'll even want to come up with Plans B, C, D, and E as backups.

Even though nobody can control all the variables in any business environment, one of the best possible strategies is to be prepared, to expect the unexpected. If you're coaching a football team, you could focus on the three plays your team performs best and drill them on just those plays until they could replicate them flawlessly, every time, no matter what.

But you wouldn't get away with that for long before the other teams' coaches caught on and came at you with plays calculated

★ ★ ★

to surprise your guys and exploit any gaps or weaknesses in your game plan. Your team would be sitting ducks because of their predictability.

On the other hand, what if you were to train the team to master a broad range of game scenarios, so that they'd be prepared to deal with practically anything that got thrown at them? No matter what happened in a game, they'd be trained to handle it. That's being prepared. That's a strategy.

It's a strategy that happens to work very, very well for the United States Marine Corps. They train soldiers for every possible scenario that could arise on the battlefield. Then they surprise you with completely new do-or-die emergency scenarios you've never seen before until you either get extremely good at adapting to anything and everything or you risk fatality.

And that brings us right back to the business battle plan. A key element of planning is to prepare for the worst as well as the best. That's the reason for having a file backup system, liability insurance, and spare car keys. Go through all the possibilities you can think of with your team and explore, "What's the worst-case scenario that could happen for us? And what's the best way to deal with that and still come out on top?"

All hands must be on deck! Everyone must be on board. Although change is inevitable, an agile organization is always prepared and trained to act strategically, not desperately. By thinking ahead, you and your team will learn to see change as an opportunity to adapt and achieve a stronger competitive edge.

Turn any business problem into an opportunity by answering four simple questions:

★ What exactly is the problem?
★ How can I fix this problem?

★ ★ ★

★ Do other people have this same problem and if so, how do they handle it?
★ Would there be people willing to buy my solution if I fix this problem?

REALITY CHECK

In order to deal with an upset situation effectively, you must let go of preconceptions about people, the market, and the economy. Start with what is actually going on before jumping to conclusions driven by fear or panic. And remember QTIP (Quit Taking It Personally)! You have to identify what the problem is before you can fix it.

Let's go back to our landscapers. Instead of looking into the reasons so many regular customers failed to renew their contracts, they panicked and reacted blindly. "We're losing customers! Better advertise to get new ones!" They ASSUMED their marketing was the problem. And you KNOW what happens when you assume, right? Assumptions get your business KILLED!

If they had taken the time to contact each of those departing customers, take a good look at their own operations, and consider local news and trends, they might have gotten their hands on some priceless market intelligence. Maybe two thirds of the customers belonged to the same Homeowners Association (HOA) and the HOA president had talked them into hiring his brother's company to do their yard work. Or maybe one of their employees was rude and unprofessional with customers and most of the ones they were losing turned out to be on her route.

Maybe their county or irrigation district had tightened up watering restrictions because of a multi-year drought, so more and more people in the area were replacing their big grassy lawns with pea gravel and cactus gardens—and our landscaper's

★ ★ ★

specialty had always been lawns. Maybe all their annual contracts were set up to expire within the same month and the landscaper had no system for sending out reminders in advance or offering early-bird discounts for advance renewals. Or it could have been that a new landscaping firm was aggressively targeting our firms' customers and offering lower rates. Understanding any of these scenarios would have given our landscapers the opportunity to regroup, develop a new strategy, and act with a clear direction and focus—to get results!

If an unexpected occurrence shakes up your world, start focusing on what really matters and on people who are on the same page as you. Revisit your core values and your company's mission or purpose. You must stay accountable for your personal actions, your team, your systems and the 20% of everything you do that gets results. Let the other 80% go, not now but right now!

Stay away from negativity and from pessimists, jealousy, complainers, and manipulators. These people are the trip wires and land mines in the business battlefield. Whenever somebody starts complaining about how nobody can make it these days because of the economy—get the hell out of that conversation and go prove them wrong.

Go back to the basics. Is your product still good? Is it still what your customers want and need? Are your customers still the market you want to be serving? Is your service superior to your competitors'?

Most importantly, take time for a reality check with yourself. Do you still believe in what you're doing? Are you doing it to the absolute best of your ability? Could YOU be the reason your business got derailed?

Take a cold, hard look around you, and get second and third opinions from people you trust and people who know more about

★ ★ ★

business than you do. Double-check your information. Figure out what the problem actually is before you decide how you're going to solve it.

COMPETITION

Up until a few years ago, advertising agencies and public relations firms called all the shots when it came to marketing. Then along came social media—like Twitter, Facebook, blogging, and YouTube. Suddenly the social media "gurus" were helping businesses reach more people through viral marketing than big, expensive ads ever could. The big agencies found out the hard way that times were changing and changing FAST. They fell behind the curve, not realizing their mistake until clients started leaking away a few at a time. They let their complacency fool them into ignoring a clear and growing trend, a trend their competitors saw coming and got prepared for.

Unless you're in a really esoteric, off-the-wall niche business, you are going to have competition. Even if you are the very first one to market with something completely original—it will only be about 20 minutes or so until somebody reverse engineers whatever you're doing and figures out a way they can do it, too, maybe even better or cheaper. That's the law of the jungle. And that's exactly how it should be.

Competition is a powerful motivator. It drives you to be the best at what you do, to cut the fat and focus on winning! It makes you accountable for staying educated, for looking ahead and learning every single day. Competition is not the real threat to your success—complacency is! And competition is the force that will not let you lapse into getting complacent.

The rules of engagement for dealing with competition are simple. Learn where they are stronger than you and fix that, NOW! Know exactly where they stand in terms of market share. Are they taking business from you or are you taking business from

★ ★ ★

them? Shop them regularly and frequently to find out exactly how they are selling their product or service and what benefits they're offering. Get every piece of marketing information from them you can get your hands on and pay close attention to what they are doing online.

Staying ahead of the competition takes constant improvement and innovation. But more than that, it takes RUTHLESS dedication to superior service. If your competitors are going after your customers or trying to undercut your prices, that doesn't mean you're dead in the water. It does mean that it's time for 5 x 5 Lima Charley loud and clear communication! Find out if you really understand what they need and want from you and make sure you're giving it to them. Educate them about the details and point out what they stand to lose by going with what might seem like a better deal from a competitor.

And always remember to keep to the high ground, because NOTHING positive will ever come out of running down your competition. No matter what, even if your client or prospect does it, taking that bait is suicide. You'll get major points by remaining respectful and professional. Point out your strengths, not your competitors' weaknesses. Show how your benefits to the client are different and better. Maintain your ethical standards at all times—no matter how much duct tape you have to strap across your lips!

At the same time, always remember that even if your competitors seem friendly, they are STILL your competitors. The phrase, "Keep your friends close and your enemies closer" relates directly to business. Watch out!

★ ★ ★

THE BUSINESS BATTLEFIELD LAW OF EQUILIBRIUM

What if you're in a field or industry and doing well for years—then all of a sudden everybody else decides to get into the same business? What if your challenge is not the kind of competition, but the sheer number of competitors out there? Does the phrase, "Real estate bubble" ring any bells for you?

If you believe in what you're doing, are excellent at doing it, and committed to staying with it, all you have to do is hold on until what I call "The Business Battlefield Law of Equilibrium" comes into play.

When a market is hot, everybody thinks they can cash in on it. Say pizza is amazingly popular in a city, so demand for pizza is up. The one pizza parlor in town is always full, with a line waiting outside, meaning there is more demand than supply. So, a couple dozen people in that city get the idea that a pizza parlor is a can't-lose idea and decide to open pizza parlors at about the same time. This reverses the situation so that there's more supply than demand. Not all of the new pizza places are going to make it—and when the Business Battlefield Law of Equilibrium swings back and evens out the supply/demand ratio again, only the ones who know what they're doing will be left standing.

Several years ago, the housing market was HOT. Prices were high and getting higher every day. Becoming a real estate agent looked like an easy way to make money to a lot of people. Suddenly, everybody was a REALTOR®—or at least everybody THOUGHT they could be a REALTOR®. In 2006 there were 5,796 licensed real estate agents in the Treasure Valley area of Idaho. Think about that—5,796 businesses of the same kind opened up in one area!

★ ★ ★

Then, the housing market tanked. Pretty soon, real estate agents were dropping out in large numbers because they couldn't get enough listings or they couldn't sell enough houses or both. By the end of 2009, the number of Treasure Valley real estate agents had dropped to 3,259. Zuber Group, a specialized real estate team, was well established before the glut of REALTORS® appeared and we rode out that wave by operating with total professionalism, great service, and sticking with our niche market until the Business Battlefield Law of Equilibrium re-established itself and cleared out the wannabes and the amateurs. We weathered the market downturn by developing a new specialty—negotiating short sales for banks—in addition to serving our niche market.

By the time things started turning around, we had little competition and plenty of product. We cleaned house!

If you find yourself surrounded by a sea of imitators, don't give up and go down. Do whatever it takes to stay afloat until THEY go down. Because most of them will, sooner than later.

THE SHORT SALE SOLUTION

In order to adapt and overcome, sometimes you've got to do certain things to get out of the trenches that you don't exactly enjoy. I understand that. As a REALTOR®, I have had to deal with banks just about every single day of my professional career, and if you think negotiating short sales with banks is fun or easy, you are dead wrong.

However, I was looking ahead and asking, "Where is this business going?" and could see a trend on the way. People were kidding themselves into these insane deals, thinking they could afford a $500,000 house on a $1500 a month payment, and lenders were giving them credit—it wasn't like this was invisible or that nobody could see it coming. The crash was all predicted,

★ ★ ★

but nobody wanted to hear it or do anything differently. And when the crash came, they got screwed!

My solution for the new reality was to switch my tactics from doing everyday real estate transactions to learning everything I could about short sales and bank-owned properties. I educated myself, becoming an expert negotiator on the bank-owned side of the deal. I convinced banks of the benefits of using my services to sell their product.

Why short sales? Because at the time, about 20% of all real estate sales in the area were short sales or bank-owned and I could visualize this number becoming much larger! I wanted to be in on that. I knew my services and skills were still valid and had value in this market—I just changed my end user. Zuber Group's systems and team and operating standards stayed the same, but our customer changed. And the best part is that the need to adapt has made my team and my business much stronger and much tougher. Our negotiating skills went through the roof.

WHAT TO KEEP AND WHAT TO CUT

When there is an economic shift, it's time to rethink, restructure, refresh, reenergize and reinvent every aspect of your business that is not getting results. Go back through your business plan, your marketing plan, your budget, and your systems to see where and how you could do more with less. You might need to retool and upgrade your systems. Are there fixed costs you could change to performance-based or bonus-based compensation?

Adapting and overcoming requires holding everything and everybody accountable. You must know what you are spending money on and what you are getting for the money spent! If any expense is not providing an adequate ROI, get rid of it. You may have to do more with a bit less, but that does not mean slashing quality or service—or your prices.

★ ★ ★

Get very clear about which aspects of your business are non-negotiable—the core of your business model, your plan and your reason for being in business in the first place. Be careful not to act in desperation and undermine the principles that make you successful in the first place. That's not adapting or overcoming, that's RETREATING.

Your commitment to excellence doesn't change. Your commitment to superior service doesn't get scaled back in any way—in fact, a down market is a powerful motivator to make you service better than ever. It forces you to do things the way you should have always been doing things.

Go back to your BBB—beans, bullets, and Band-Aids. When I was on active duty as a Marine, we'd get hand-me-down gear from the Army, so stuff was broken and beat up and we had to adapt to that reality. It was a case of fix it, tie it, duct-tape it, figure it out, make it work, shut up and do what you're here to do! No excuses!

ADAPT AND OVERCOME CHECKLIST

★ Become an expert on your product and service, right now!
★ Educate yourself monthly on the current market conditions and surrounding environment.
★ Understand the needs of your prospects/clients in the current conditions.
★ Become an avid student of what your competition is doing right and what you believe they're doing wrong.
★ Hold every expense accountable.
★ Surround yourself with successful business owners and positive people.
★ Know and understand your personal values! What do you need? What do you want?
★ Focus on the 20% that matters and let the rest go!
★ Become an expert at lead generation.

★ ★ ★

* ★ Track and measure everything!
* ★ Retool or upgrade your systems.
* ★ Hire a coach or get involved with a training program or mastermind group that will hold you accountable.

STAND OUT—BY BEING THE BEST!

Never blend in. Camouflaging yourself in business is not a freaking option—whatever it takes, ethically, to stand out is what you need to do. And what's the number-one best way to differentiate you from all competitors? Be the best. Mediocrity and blending in are for losers. Not taking risks and always playing it safe = MEDIOCRITY. Being average might feel safe and comfortable, but SAFE = INVISIBLE and INVISIBLE = OUT OF BUSINESS!

Take an honest look in the mirror and ask yourself hard questions. Are you maximizing your own productivity? Are you focusing on what matters most or spinning your wheels? Are you doing what you get paid to do? Running a business demands that you prove yourself over and over again, every day. Tenure, credentials, and years of experience do not substitute for results. No one is paying you to pace yourself or budget your efforts.

Eliminate distractions and cut tactics that aren't working. Push harder than you've ever pushed before. Start getting exceptionally good at the basics of business success, like closing, marketing, and negotiating by dedicating time and discipline to educate yourself and practice, practice, practice. Becoming better isn't good enough—become the best!

Your life can be about your problems or your opportunities. You can choose to either run away from what you fear or start running toward what you want. Expect great things to happen—and then go make them happen!

★ ★ ★

ADAPT AND OVERCOME TOP 5 TAKEAWAYS

Take the time to do a reality check and understand what the problem is before you start fixing it.

1. Cutting expenses does not mean slashing quality or delivering less.
2. The best way to stand out from the competition is to be the BEST.
3. In a saturated market, hang tough until the Business Battlefield Law of Equilibrium weeds out the faint-hearted.
4. Competition is not the real threat to your success—complacency is.

YOUR MARCHING ORDERS

Call your top five customers and ask them, "What are we doing right? What is one thing we could do better? What is it that makes you choose to do business with us instead of somebody else?"

★ ★ ★

COMBAT TRAINING

★ ★ ★

EDUCATE YOURSELF AND YOUR CLIENTS. YOUR FUTURE DEPENDS ON IT!

"Formal education will make you a living;
self-education will make you a fortune."
– Jim Rohn

Nobody wins in the business trenches without knowing their territory and making the most of every experience in order to become tougher, smarter, and more effective. This chapter covers the extreme importance of education on an as-needed basis and shows you how to quickly educate yourself when time is of the essence. Self-education is about searching and finding answers that count—even in a so-called "dead end job" there is valuable experience and knowledge to be gained and leveraged.

What this chapter won't cover is traditional, formal education or how a college degree applies to business success. Education is never free. You pay for it one way or another, so it makes sense to evaluate whether the benefits outweigh the costs whether it's $200,000 to attend Harvard, a dozen years of trial and error, or $19.95 for a book like this one. There are so many resources and opportunities available today for smart, motivated, driven

★ ★ ★

entrepreneurs to educate themselves—some at little or no cost—ranging from free online videos to pricey private coaching. If what you don't know is hurting your business, you better figure out a way to start knowing it! Or surround yourself with people who do and can help you.

EDUCATION DEFINED

When people hear the word "education," they tend to think of formal education, as in universities and degree requirements and GPAs and exams and long, pointless lectures about somebody who died 350 years ago. In a country that no longer exists.

But when I say education, what I'm mainly talking about is self-education. Formal education is institutionalized learning where they feed you a certain amount of material from a predetermined menu. There are general education requirements and core classes that may or may not ever pertain to what you're going to actually DO for the rest of your life.

Self-education is another thing altogether. It's about learning on your own terms and your own timeline. It's when you're the one who initiates it and you actively go and seek out the specific skills or knowledge that will make you a better businessperson. Self-education means paying attention and sometimes learning the hard way. It's figuring it out, looking it up, developing street smarts, or finding someone who knows what they're doing and asking them how they do it. It's about being able to identify where the gaps are and closing them up.

Now, don't get me wrong, I am definitely not knocking formal education. Anybody who earns any kind of degree has every right to be very proud of that accomplishment. In the big picture, higher education can make for a richer life experience in so many ways, and in certain fields (such as law and medicine) it's mandatory. My son, Zac wants to become a Blue Angel fighter pilot when he grows up, and for that he'll need to go to college.

★ ★ ★

But we are entrepreneurs, in the trenches, where education has life-or-death urgency! Here in the business trenches, you can't pause the movie and take a time-out. You must learn in action while you're still running the business. You need to earn while you learn. You need to find out what it is you don't know that's getting you killed and learn it RIGHT NOW so you can start using it and start winning.

Bottom line is this: You do not need a college degree to succeed in business. You absolutely DO need to educate yourself, on an ongoing basis, to succeed in business.

BENEFITS OF EDUCATION

Education gives you your marching orders—clear direction about what to do next and how. Start here, this is it.

There's no substitute for the confidence that comes from knowing what you're talking about. And that confidence makes all the difference in everything an entrepreneur needs to do to win, from being a leader to making tough decisions to negotiating and closing a deal. Without confidence, you are DEAD.

By improving your knowledge and skills and AWARENESS, you make yourself better and that translates into better business results. It's the foundation for making more money and getting the results you want both now and later on down the road. If you lack a good foundation or a good grasp of the business basics, then it's costing you money every single day.

In any small business, the owner's weaknesses telescope out and become the business's weaknesses. They become the holes where revenue and opportunities leak away. So by making yourself the best that you can be or by hiring somebody who excels at what you're weakest in, and either hiring them or learning from them, you're plugging those holes.

★ ★ ★

With self-education, you learn by doing and the doing can start RIGHT NOW.

TEN TIPS FOR GETTING EDUCATED RIGHT NOW!

1. Go to Google and do your own research. If you're not getting the answers you need, ask the questions differently.
2. Read blogs and forums. There are so many blogs on just about every topic these days that you can get reasonably up to speed on your subject in an afternoon.
3. Watch informational or training videos on YouTube.
4. Browse bookstore magazine racks for industry-specific articles and trends.
5. Watch Webinars and listen to Podcasts.
6. Subscribe to Google Alerts for regular news updates on what's being posted about your subject.
7. Hire a business coach.
8. Take a community education class or a subscription-training program.
9. Sign up for a seminar, presentation, or workshop on your subject.
10. Buy books—and READ them and ACT ON what you learn.

SELF-EDUCATION IN ACTION

Let me give you an example of learning in action. My real estate business, Zuber Group, had reached a new level of efficiency and productivity. We had the right people on a great team. We had excellent systems in place and our service was incredible. My negotiating and closing skills were way above par and I had been steadily growing my sphere of influence. But, that sphere wasn't large enough at the time to support the volume of sales we were capable of.

★ ★ ★

The phone wasn't ringing often enough to support my commitments to my team. I had to do something, and quickly. There wasn't time to go back to school and get a degree in marketing or advertising—but I needed to become much better at making the phone the ring, generating more opportunities and more at-bats.

The plan: I made a commitment to the team and myself that I would become a marketing expert within the next 30 days.

I went to grocery stores and stood in check out lines to see which magazines popped out at me and grabbed my attention. What was it about People magazine and National Enquirer that was so irresistible you had to pick them up and take a closer look? It was the HEADLINES. "Katie collapses before wedding to Tom," or "Marie Osmond's suicide attempt." Who knows why we all find this so fascinating, but it WORKS!

I spent time browsing Barnes & Noble's large display of magazines as well. When you are staring at 500 hundred magazines at a time, what makes a certain few stand out? The colors—especially yellows and reds—and bold fonts. When combined with WORDS that that were also bold and colorful, the headlines really popped. WOW! I was beginning to pick up on this.

I spent roughly $50 on books about effective marketing, advertising methods, and especially, how to write head-turning, eyeball-grabbing headlines.

I went to the Internet, searched blogs, and studied what larger companies like NIKE and McDonalds were doing. I bought multiple Sunday papers and pored over every page of the advertising inserts to see which ads grabbed my attention. The ads offering something "FREE" and "100% satisfaction GUARANTEED" always stood out the most.

★ ★ ★

We put all this knowledge to work in our signage and began to get results immediately. Zuber Group's incoming call volume was soon up to five times more calls than we'd ever had. My self-education took less than a month, cost very little money, and paid off fast.

KNOW WHAT YOU NEED TO KNOW

At a minimum, every business owner needs to stay knowledgeable about:

★ The basics of how to run a business
★ Market conditions
★ What the competition is doing
★ Industry trends
★ Lead generation

It's also critical to continually improve and update your skills. That could be selling skills, communication skills, leadership skills, writing skills, public speaking skills—even new software skills. If you're a bike mechanic, you better know how to work on the latest models. If you're a graphic designer, you better be an expert with InDesign, or whatever design software your clients and vendors are working in.

How can you learn everything you need to know? By starting with what's most important and building from there. Nothing is static in life or in business. Market conditions shift, perceptions change, the economy goes through cycles, technology evolves, generations keep coming in wave after wave. The secret is to pay attention, enjoy the ride, and make continuous education a life-long habit.

★ ★ ★

EDUCATION RETURN ON INVESTMENT (ROI)

We all know that time is money. So it makes zero sense to spend either one unless you're sure of getting a substantial return on your investment (ROI). With education, everything should be about the ROI. Not only how much does this cost and how much will it help me earn, but also how soon will I recoup that investment?

Start by establishing a ratio. For example, let's say I decide my benchmark is a return of three times my investment. That means for every dollar I spend I expect to make three dollars in return—a reasonable expectation for a business decision. With that 3:1 ratio in mind, if I invest $100,000 in a college education for the purpose of getting a great job, can I reasonably expect to make $300,000 as a result? And if so, how long will it take? If the average job out there is paying $30,000 then recouping my investment would take ten years. Ten years is too long! At minimum, I want to see at least a 3-to-1 ratio of return-to-investment within one year. I'm not willing to risk $50,000 unless I'm confident I'm going to make at least $150,000.

The great thing about self-education is that it almost always comes with a kick-ass payback. A $20 book can make you a 30:1 return on investment if it helps you save or make as little as $600.

Inexpensive, even free, educational opportunities are readily available all over the place. In a very short amount of time you can buy and read three books on any business subject for $15 each, download and read an e-book for $20, and attend a brief workshop, podcast, or webinar for $35. All of that information for only $100! You could easily make ten times your investment back, not three (depending on what it is you're selling, of course), on your next sale. The very next day. If you wanted to

★ ★ ★

become better educated on ten specific topics using the same game plan, you'd still only be spending a total of $1,000. Now THAT is an investment worth making.

RAMP IT UP—LEARN FROM THE EXPERTS!

One of the best ways to get the most dramatic improvement in the shortest amount of time is to hire a business coach. Elite athletes don't attempt to do everything on their own or stumble along by trial-and-error—their time is too precious to piss around like that. Elite athletes ALWAYS have personal coaches for very good reasons. Even amateur athletes who are serious about getting superior results, fast, hire personal trainers and coaches.

Why? Because getting expert support on the planning, strategizing, and troubleshooting frees them up to devote 100% to DOING and ACHIEVING. And the one-on-one attention means that every step large or small is tailored to their needs, designed to maximize their unique strengths and eliminate their unique weaknesses.

With the right business coach or trainer you can skip right past the learning curve of having to figure out how to apply the theory you're learning to what you actually need to accomplish. Instead, you get one-on-one advice and analysis from an expert who is 100% dedicated to your day-to-day actions and results.

EDUCATE YOUR CLIENTS

Another PRICELESS benefit of educating yourself is that it allows you to position yourself as a superstar in your clients' eyes. You become a trusted advisor instead of an annoying salesperson. By giving your clients and customers important, interesting, relevant information about your industry in general you earn their trust. Let's face it—we all avoid salespeople. Most people these days are suspicious of advertising and can smell a sales pitch coming a mile away.

★ ★ ★

144

But—we seek out trusted advisors.

As a business professional, you have a responsibility to educate your clients. That does not mean you bore them with long, complex lectures; the idea is to help them understand what they need to know about your industry or the market to make decisions that are in their best interest.

Keep in mind that you are the expert and they're not—that's why they need you. You have all the background and know the ins and outs of your product or service or process—they don't. That can be intimidating. It's your job to help them get comfortable enough to move forward with confidence—or to decide not to move forward if that turns out to be a better decision for them.

In the real estate business, I sell my services every day. I work with clients who might only buy or sell 2 -3 houses in their entire lives. Unless they've done a lot of research, they may not even know what escrow is, or what a short sale is. They don't know what they don't know, so a big part of my service—and the main reason my service is so valuable—is educating them about what they need to know to take part in the game. Buying or selling a house is a complicated process. It's a decision they'll have to live with for years to come, so I owe it to them to make sure they know what they're doing and signing.

If you're well educated and well informed, you are able to give your clients and prospects and even your colleagues GREAT value without having to sell them anything. They can let down their guard and build a genuine relationship with you, completely free of any nagging obligation to buy anything from you. So when it does come time to buy, guess who they'll turn to?

In other chapters, we've talked a lot about how critical it is to ask clients the right questions, not only about their needs and pain points and desires, but also questions that explore what they

★ ★ ★

know about your area of expertise. Before you bring up any big questions, make damn sure you know the answer! The more you know, the more you can alleviate their fears and help them make sound decisions that really are in their best interests.

Educating clients is an indispensable part of the business relationship, and one that many, many business owners fail to take advantage of. So jump in and fill that gap! Learn everything you can that will equip you to be THE go-to resource for your clients, and pretty soon this tactic will have them asking for your help, instead of you having to close them!

LEARNING IN ACTION—EVERY EXPERIENCE COUNTS!

Education equals experience in business. Amassing knowledge is only the first step. Putting it into practice is what will keep you alive. And EVERY experience in life—good and bad—is a golden learning opportunity.

If you crash and burn, make time to do an autopsy on what happened, dissecting every step all the way from the beginning. Almost always there is something that could have been done better. What went wrong? How could you have done it differently? What fell through the cracks? What got overlooked or stressed too heavily? What would you change if you had the chance to do it over?

Same goes for successes—take time to evaluate why it worked and how to make it work repeatedly and consistently from now on. Revisit every step and look for ways to make it even better than great next time.

Even a job at McDonalds—one that most people consider a "dead end job"—will teach you about at least a dozen business functions: systems, marketing, organization, customer relationship management, problem-solving, teamwork, inventory

★ ★ ★

control, branding, the list goes on and on. Even if the only lesson you learn is that you're not cut out for food service, that's still valuable information, better learned sooner than later.

Learning through experience is the best way to learn, by taking the time to reflect and analyze what went down. And how. And why. I'm the first one to admit that I have failed many times and made many mistakes. I wrote this book to help you avoid those mistakes. That's where the big learning comes from, right there. Learning comes from how you handle failing.

A deal might not have closed, or maybe a transaction failed to go the way everybody involved expected it to go. But about 95% of the time, there is something you could have done that would have made it work better. But there is still the 5% of the time that even doing every possible thing right won't make it play out the way you want it to. When that happens, and when you can honestly say you did everything within your control you could have done—let it go and move on. Might not be easy, but let it go. Leave it where it fell, knock the dirt off your back, and rise to meet the next adventure.

MARINES APPROACH TO COMBAT TRAINING

Combat training is invasive, intense, urgent, loud, brutal and IN YOUR FACE. Military experts have designed it that way 100% intentionally to scare the shit out of you and get your attention and make every lesson stick. And they don't teach it in a classroom, you have to experience it in your bones and your straining muscles and your sweat and your adrenaline and your fear so that you learn how powerful and capable a human being can be, even in extreme conditions.

Combat training is designed to simulate actual battle conditions and make you repeat the desired behavior over and

★ ★ ★

over and over so that you can produce that desired behavior UNDER FIRE. Does it suck? Does it hurt? Does it rip you apart emotionally, mentally, and physically? Hell, yes.

So why endure it? Because it's the only way to stay ALIVE in the trenches. You absolutely MUST have the skills of battle down so well that you can perform the right steps in the right order no matter what is going on around you. When you're a soldier, you learn under duress. You learn by repetition. YOU LEARN BECAUSE YOU HAVE TO. You learn when to react, when not to react, and how to react. You become prepared to respond—proficiently—to whatever gets thrown at you. Anybody can perform well in a safe, comfortable environment, but when the bullets are flying and casualties are mounting—that's when it counts. That's when and where education pays off.

There is another aspect of combat training that is also critical in business training—it must be practiced and put into action. Reading about it isn't enough, getting a certificate isn't enough, knowing it isn't even enough. You've got to be able to apply it in action and keep practicing it to remain capable of peak performance at all times.

Like athletic training and combat training, business training conditions you to do what you need to do without even thinking about it. The right action becomes second nature, and business performance becomes a habit, and that frees your mind to FOCUS on the bigger picture and the vision that will dramatically boost your results.

★ ★ ★

COMBAT TRAINING TOP 5 TAKEAWAYS

1. Every experience counts! There is no such thing as a dead-end job.
2. You must educate yourself on an ongoing basis to succeed in business.
3. Educate your clients so that you become a trusted advisor in their eyes—as opposed to a salesperson.
4. With self-education, you learn by doing, and that doing can start RIGHT NOW.
5. Knowledge is power! There is no substitute for the confidence that comes from knowing what you're talking about.

YOUR MARCHING ORDERS

Congratulations—by purchasing and reading this book, you have already taken a huge step in educating yourself to be the best you can be on the business battlefield! Now it's time for another step.

How would it boost your business results if you became at expert at lead generation, closing, negotiation, financial planning, or systems? Based on the natural talent and experience you've already got, which one of these areas of expertise would you be best able to master in the shortest amount of time?

Schedule three (or more!) action steps you can take in the next 30 days to learn more about it or get more practice doing it, or both!

★ ★ ★

SEMPER FI

★ ★ ★

NEVER, EVER, EVER GIVE UP!

The human spirit is never finished when it's defeated.
It's finished when it surrenders.
– Ben Stein

What are you willing to die for? If it came to that, what would you not be able to stop doing, no matter what the consequences? Think about that for a while, write down what rises to the top of your list of what matters in life, and then compare it to your current actions. Do they match? If not, fix it—NOW!

"Semper Fidelis" has been the motto of the United States Marine Corps since 1883. It translates as "Always Faithful." Not "relatively faithful," or "faithful when I feel like it," but ALWAYS!

In this changing business world, commitment means remaining steadfast and true to your core values, no matter how much shit is thrown in the path in front of you. It means reminding yourself of your obligations—not just to other people but to yourself and to your business—and honoring them, no excuses.

★★★

CORE VALUES OF THE U.S. MARINE CORPS
★ HONOR
★ COURAGE
★ COMMITMENT

Generations of American men and women have given special meaning to the title "United States Marine." They live by these enduring principles, which form the bedrock of their character, give them strength, and guide their decisions and actions. These values bond the USMC into a united force capable of meeting any challenge.

COMMITMENT

In the beginning of this book I gave you my take on the idea of setting a goal vs. making a commitment. A goal is a "someday" thing. Commitment is about what you will actually DO, today—NOW!—and every day after that for as long as it takes. Dreams and goals are fine, but they will not do you any good or get you anywhere without ACTION.

Commitment is 100% based on action. It's about doing, not just saying. Commitment is the twin of discipline—doing what you know must be done whether you feel like it or not. A committed man or woman follows through, living what they profess, acting on their truth.

There is no room on the business battlefield for dropouts—people who start something and then quit when it becomes difficult or inconvenient. There is no room for cop-outs—people who have no mission, no purpose, and no hunger for greatness. And there is definitely no room for holdouts—people who sit forever on the fence, who can't decide if they're more afraid of failing or succeeding, so they never commit.

★ ★ ★

There are dozens of sayings about fence sitters: On the bus or off the bus! Shit or get off the pot! Are you in or are you out? The time to hesitate is past! It's now or never! All of these sayings hold true because it's been well understood for thousands of years that commitment is not a half-hearted thing. Commitment is all or nothing, black or white, DO or DIE!

Picture yourself on the verge of stepping on board a boat, a boat that's bobbing in the tide and about to drift away. How long do you think you can balance with one foot on the wharf and one foot on the boat before you fall in? How will it feel if you chicken out and you're left on the shore watching your boat sail out of sight without you?

Commitment is the key to unlocking doors and windows and letting the light shine in to show you how to lead a more focused life. And it starts within the heart. Your heart can carry you the distance even when all your other vital organs and resources have begun to fail.

YOUR PURPOSE—CORE VALUES

Winning in the trenches requires commitment to your core values. There's got to be a powerful, driving reason for your business to exist and for YOU to be the one at the wheel. Of course, a business exists to make money, but you'll need a hell of a lot more than just the profit motive to get you out of bed every morning and keep you and your team going when you're under fire.

If you're in a business you're not passionate about, it's time to ask yourself why. Doing something you don't believe in makes no sense. Nor is it fair to your family, the people you surround yourself with, your clients, your employer, or your employees. They all deserve your best. Being half-assed in your work is pointless. If you don't love it, why are you doing it? And if you DO love it, what's holding you back from being the best at it?

★ ★ ★

For all of us in any business, core values are not descriptions of the work we do or the strategies we use to get things done. Core values are the principles that UNDERLIE everything else; they govern how we interact with people and guide the practices we use (or better be using!) every day in everything we do.

Honor, courage, excellence, loyalty, honesty, family, country—whatever is on your top priority list of core values is what gives meaning and purpose to your life and work.

Core values:

- ★ Govern personal relationships.
- ★ Guide business decisions.
- ★ Clarify who we are as people and business people.
- ★ Articulate what our business stands for.
- ★ Explain why we do business the way we do.
- ★ Inform the way we lead, teach, and reward others.

So—why exactly are you doing this? What—and who—matters to you so much that NOTHING could stop you? If you are a true entrepreneur those are the world's easiest questions to answer.

HARNESS FEAR!

Courage is not the absence of fear, courage is pushing on through even if you're scared shitless. For every Marine and every individual in every branch of the armed forces, a no-excuses commitment to courage under fire is 100% mandatory. And 100% delivered, proudly.

Combat training and endless drills are relentless for a reason—to hammer home the habit of mastering your instinctive reactions. It gets pounded into you until you absolutely KNOW you WILL do the right thing with precision and consistency NO

★ ★ ★

MATTER WHAT. Not only is your mind committed, your body and reflexes are well trained to execute as you will them to.

Fear is a powerful force—it fills your body with adrenaline and makes every sense come alive to peak alertness. And you can harness that force and use it! Fight or flight, right? That means you can choose to fight instead of retreating.

You can leverage your fear and turn it into positive energy, because dread can be one hell of a motivator. In fact, I used it to get your attention in the very first line of this book, "What would you do differently—RIGHT NOW—if you knew your life depended on it?"

Fear of a head-on collision will make you pay attention to the road. Fear of flunking out could make you study enough to ace the test. Fear of looking like an idiot will make you learn your lines for that speech, no matter how late you have to stay up to do it. Fear of going bankrupt could finally motivate you to put business systems in place and go the extra mile to make dead sure your customers are ecstatic, not just happy.

Let's say I have an employee who's been getting away with coasting on the job. I walk into the office one morning and say to him, "Look, we're going to have to cut your salary or put you on a commission-only basis. We're going to have to do something different, starting right now, because you need to close at least four transactions in the next month or we won't be able to keep you here."

At this point, I can assure you this person is scared to death, and one of three things will happen next. The conversation may have lit a fire under their ass that motivates them to figure out and execute every possible step they can take to keep their job. Or, they realize they hate their job and they hate me so they'll call anybody and everybody they can think of to find a different

★ ★ ★

job. Those two possibilities are both prime examples of using fear as a motivator.

But there is that third possibility: they could choose flight over fight and simply give up and wait for the axe to fall. Fear can be a paralyzing force as well as a motivating force. Fear can make you choke at exactly the wrong second—if you let it.

It's your choice.

THE BUCK STOPS WITH YOU

Have you ever known somebody who keeps moving from job to job or from city to city because no matter where they go, it's never right? There's always something that's just not quite right and they can't put their finger on it. But you can if you've known them long enough—the problem is them. Wherever they go, they have to take themselves with them. And they keep pulling the same old shit and getting the same old results and blaming everything and everyone but themselves for the outcome.

There is no end of excuses out there and people come up with new ones every day. You ask, "How's business?" And they shake their heads and tell you it's lousy. If you go on to ask, "How come?" invariably they have some reason that's completely outside their control. It's the economy. It's tax time and nobody's spending money. It's summer/winter/spring break/the holidays. It's my spouse/kids/in-laws. It's this crazy weather. It's the Democrats/the Republicans. It's the media. It's this town. It's my suppliers/customers/employees—they're all crooks. And on and on and on. There are plenty of boo-hooers out there.

We can all point fingers and play the blame game. But if you don't like your job, whose fault is that? The only person who can make you give up on yourself or your long-term strategy is YOU. The only person who can change your life, your career, or your business results is YOU.

★ ★ ★

If the problem is your boss—fix it. Go to her and speak up about it. If 10 customers cancel their orders in the same week, do you think it's because they all turned into jerks at the same time for no good reason? Or could it be something you're doing or not doing? ASK THEM. Business owners who take responsibility for making things right make a big impression, in ANY economy.

FAILURE IS ONLY TEMPORARY

Complacency is the enemy of performance. When I start getting comfortable, I know it's time to raise the bar, shake things up, and take a risk. By definition, risk means the outcome is not guaranteed and there's a real possibility that whatever it is you're daring to do might not work. Any entrepreneur who makes it big will experience failure along the way, probably multiple times.

But keep in mind that big successes involve taking big risks; so doing things differently will mean falling on your face at times. And when that happens, you will get right back up, figure out how to do better next time, and get back in the game.

Quitting is not an option. Giving up for the wrong reasons is not an option. But failure is part of the territory. You do everything you can to prevent it of course, by focusing on everything within your control and letting the rest go.

To get anywhere or learn anything, you must take risks, and that means risking failure. When you learn to snowboard or wakeboard, you'll end up falling down over and over again until you get it right. The only way to completely avoid failure is to completely avoid any kind of risk. There will be plenty of time for that when you are DEAD. And if you are so paralyzed by fear that you're trying to live a risk-free life then you might as well be dead. Where is the thrill in that? The satisfaction? Failures are learning opportunities and each one is just another step on the ladder to where you're headed.

★ ★ ★

Failing is like getting a "no" answer during a negotiation; it's only temporary. It's only an opportunity to listen better, learn more, and ask again in a different way.

Getting knocked down hurts, but it also galvanizes you to do better, to go for it just that much harder to make sure you don't get knocked down next time. When determination to win takes over the fear of failure, you'll know what I'm talking about. OOH-RAH!

IT'S YOUR FLIGHT, SOLDIER— SO ENJOY IT!

Being the best that you can be, making and keeping commitments, and staying "Forever Faithful" to your core values are all essential ingredients for running a bulletproof business and getting out of the trenches.

It's hard work and it takes guts and discipline—but it is also one hell of a great ride! If running a business were easy everybody would be doing it, because just about everybody secretly wants to. Who doesn't dream of running their own show? Who wouldn't rather call the shots than dodge somebody else's misfired bullets? While others on the nine-to-five treadmill are slogging through their days, entrepreneurs are going for the prize.

Some of us were just not meant to work for somebody else, and even if working for ourselves means working ten times harder, we wouldn't have it any other way.

My friend, Ensign J.T. Bolt (a commissioned Navy officer) told me a story one day that sums it all up beautifully.

As a boy growing up in Idaho I had long dreamed of becoming a US Navy pilot. I was told several times that my dream was a fantasy; that I did not possess the skills, talent or aptitude to achieve such a demanding goal.

★ ★ ★

I persisted through the years and eventually found myself in US Navy flight school, pursuing my dream. But this is where the real story begins. Because flight school was not the dream I had imagined it to be. It was tough. It was nonstop arduous study, demanding written and oral exams, and constant flight evaluations. Each flight was demanding. We were graded on every aspect, from preparation and execution to debrief. The criteria were strict and the instructors were unrelenting in their demands for excellence.

One day, I was flying with a new instructor, a man whom I had never met prior to that day's flight. I was very nervous, wound up tight, and in heavy anticipation of his onslaught of questions. Oh yeah, and we were about to execute procedures like recovery from intentional engine failure, spins, and a litany of in-flight emergency procedures.

As we flew down the Texas coastline on our way to the block of airspace designated for the demanding flight procedures we were about to perform, I looked in the rear-view mirrors mounted on the aircraft's canopy rails. There, in the back seat, I observed my flight instructor, calmly and confidently sitting with helmet donned, dark visor covering his eyes, oxygen mask pulled to one side displaying a satisfying smile as he scanned the sky. "Man, it's too bad you guys are getting graded on this," he said over the intercom, "You just have no idea how frickin' cool this is!"

His point sank in immediately. We were military pilots. We were pursuing our passion, our dreams. And despite the demands and stress of the profession, there were hoards of people who would kill to be in our position. I had friends who had attempted flight training and either failed to qualify or washed out. And here I was, living the dream but barely taking a moment to appreciate it.

This lesson has remained with me in business. It is easy to dream of business success, financial windfalls and overflowing prosperity when we first get the idea to start a business. As budding entrepreneurs, we (like flight school students) rarely imagine the challenges, setbacks and frustrations that come with the territory of entrepreneurship.

★ ★ ★

The most important lesson I have learned from both flight school and business is to take some time each day to enjoy the flight; appreciate the gift of the pursuit of your dreams. Realize that there are millions of people who are enslaved by their employment, perhaps unqualified to be chasing the dream of being in business for themselves. Know that several have failed, simply by giving up.

And while there are no flight instructors breathing down your neck in business, you will be the toughest judge ever of your own performance.

Success in the business trenches or in life doesn't come from where you born, it doesn't come from how you where raised or where you went to school. It doesn't come from some lucky break or depend on whether you are smarter than the next person. Success comes from commitment to your long-term strategy. It comes from refusing to abandon the quest and pushing on through the moments when quitting would be so much easier.

So fly your airplane. Run your business, because YOU are in the pilot's seat. Do you have any idea how frickin' cool that is?

★ ★ ★

ABOUT THE AUTHOR

★ ★ ★

Craig Zuber is a business coach, author, speaker, top-producer in residential real estate, creator of the Business Combat Training Program, and most importantly—a Marine.

Zuber grew up in central California and started his first business at age 10, selling candy to classmates using his school locker as a storefront. He did well right through 7th grade, until the school realized how much his operation was directly affecting their bottom line and shut it down.

As president of Zuber Group, Inc., Zuber currently leads one of Idaho's most successful real estate teams.

During his very first year in real estate, Zuber made $9.8 million in sales. How? By taking everything he learned in the United States Marine Corps and translating that discipline and life-or-death execution to business success.

A born competitor, Zuber was a 1st team all-league MVP in baseball during high school, even once playing against Alex Rodriguez in Reggie Jackson's Upper Deck Classic tournament.

★★★

He turned down a baseball scholarship to join the Marines in 1993. He enlisted in the US Marine Corps to serve the country he loves, the best nation on Earth, the land of opportunity where anyone is free to become whatever he or she is determined to be. Military principles and discipline left an indelible mark on Zuber's life and business practices.

Nobody gets to the top alone. Zuber could not have made it without the courage, vision, and sheer grit of his partner in work and in life, Nicole Zuber. Not only did Nicole support her husband's move into real estate, she charged right in with him, becoming a realtor herself, learning the ropes, researching markets, zeroing in on the best place to create a thriving business and raise their children. The couple now resides in Boise, Idaho, where they are the proud parents of Zac (6) and Aspen (3).

Zuber has been spending a lot of his time championing the cause of seeing military personnel effectively transition into the workplace once they leave active duty. There are nearly 500,000 individuals annually who find themselves in this position. With their leadership and training, Zuber believes that many of them have the abilities to be successful entrepreneurs and business leaders. Zuber's mission is to provide them with a little guidance to uncover 10 entrepreneurial principles that they learned in the military – and how to directly apply them to business ownership.

Zuber is determined to make sure their business is the next blockbuster success story, not the next casually.

★ ★ ★

BEHIND THE EMBLEM

★ ★ ★

Symbolizing those who have been in the trenches in the past, are currently in the trenches, and those who are about to step onto the business battlefield.

COMMITMENT
We never give up, never give in, and never willingly accept second best.

COURAGE
We keep pushing on through even if we're scared shitless.

ACCOUNTABILITY
We do what we say we're going to do.

VICTORY
We win as a team by developing exceptional service.

LEADERSHIP
We lead by example.

BACKGROUND

Vital Stats:

Name: Luis Santa
Email: bigrican@live.com
Age: 35
Height: 5'6"
Weight: 165 1/4 lbs
Years Bodybuilding: 16

Military Background:

Branch Of Service: Air Force
Years Of Service: 8
Rank: Ssgt/E-5
MOS: 3D0X1/ Knowledge Operations
Manager

HOW DID YOU GET STARTED?

I started working out through the encouragement of a good friend. Though already ripped and physically fit, he said I would benefit from having more muscle mass. I have been involved in many sports throughout my life: Karate, distance running, gymnastics and baseball are just a few. I gave bodybuilding a shot and immediately became hooked.

CIVILIAN LIFE TO MILITARY LIFE
What Is The Hardest Part?

The liberties in civilian life are definitely not the same in the military. Being able to make my own choices vs. being told what to do was the hardest transition for me. The military's great structure taught me to become more disciplined and focused. Integrity first, service before self, and excellence in everything I do are core values that have helped me in life and the sport of bodybuilding.

WORKOUT PLAN

Monday - Chest:
Flat Dumbbell Press: 4 sets of 10-12 reps
Incline Bench Press: 3 sets of 10-12 reps
Decline Bench Press: 3 sets of 10-12 reps

Tuesday - Arms:
Straight Bar Curls: 4 sets of 10-12 reps
Alternate Dumbbell Curls: 3 sets of 10-12 reps
Straight Bar 21s: 3 sets of 7, 7, 7 reps
Skull Crushers: 4 sets of 10-12 reps
Bench Press Close-Grip Presses: 3 sets of 10-12 reps
One-Arm Cable Push-Downs: 3 sets of 15 reps

Wednesday - Legs:
Hack Squats: 4 sets of 10-12 reps
Leg Extensions: 3 sets of 10-12 reps
Stiff Leg Dead Lifts: 3 sets of 10-12 reps
One-Leg Hamstring Curls: 3 sets of 10-12 reps
Abductor Machine: 3 sets of 25 reps
Seated Calf Raises: 4 sets of 15 reps
Leg-Press Machine Calf Presses: 4 sets of 15 reps

Friday - Shoulders:
Military Dumbbell Press: 4 sets of 10-12 reps
Upright Rows: 3 sets of 10-12 reps
Dumbbell Lateral Raises: 3 sets of 10-12 reps
Barbell Shrugs (Front): 4 sets of 12 reps
Barbell Shrugs (Back): 4 sets of 12 reps

Saturday - Back:
Pull-Ups: 3 sets of 10-12 reps
Seated Cable Rows: 4 sets of 10-12 reps
Cable Lateral Pull-Downs: 3 sets of 10-12 reps
Bent-Over Rows: 3 sets of 10-12 reps

Note: I do workout rotations of 3 days on, one day off. It does not matter which day you start your rotation, but you will not do the same workout on the same day, and you will not have the same days off either.

NUTRITION PLAN

0515
Wake up, and get ready for work.

0630
3/4 Cup Of Oatmeal Cooked In Water

0800
10 Egg Whites
One Yolk
2 Slices Of Ezekiel Low Sodium Bread

0930
8oz Of Chicken Breast
1 Cup Cooked Brown Rice

1100
1 Granny Apple

1230
8oz Of Chicken
A Baked Potato

1400
1 Cup Green Grapes

1530
Protein Shake With Pre-Workout Supplement Prior To Workout

1800
Protein Shake With Post-Workout Supplement

1930
8-12oz Of Chicken Breast
1 Cup Brown Rice

2100
8oz Of Chicken Breast

2200
In bed, knocked out.

SUPPLEMENTS

Multi-vitamin
Muscle Asylum Project - Arson
Potassium (aside from multi-vitamin)
Magnesium (aside from multi-vitamin)
Zinc (aside from multi-vitamin)
NO-Shotgun (pre-workout)
NO-SyntheSize (post-workout)
Muscle Milk Light (chocolate)
Vitamin C
CLA
Flaxseed Oil